The Complete Beginner's Guide to Companion Planting

Natural Gardening Techniques That Save Time and Money to
Achieve Year-Round Bountiful Harvests

by
Anita Greensong

Contents

Introduction

Plant parsley and asparagus together, and you'll have more of each, but keep broccoli and tomato plants far apart if you want them to thrive.

Louise Riotte

A gardener's heart ached as she looked out on her garden. Her vegetables were wilting. They were drooped like flags on a still day. The abundance that she was promised seemed almost like a joke now. The magazines she looked at had told her that she'd have overflowing baskets and gorgeous blooms, but this was far from it. What had she done wrong? She read all the books and followed the schedules to a tee but remained confused. Did her soil need amending? Did she sow her seeds too early? Too late? The more she thought about it, the more information overwhelmed her.

Indecision was not her friend, but space was also an enemy. Her tiny patio left little room for experimentation, and the resources she had were stretched thin. She had to balance work with her daily chores, and now she had garden maintenance, which made it feel impossible. Just when she had the energy to weed her garden, aphids descended. They seemed to make fun of her, and the sign was in the chewed-up leaves. Her dream of having fresh, homegrown food was fading, quickly being replaced with the pangs of failure. She felt like gardening was for those who had nothing but time on their hands, lots of land, and an endless budget.

There had to be a simpler way. Something had to exist out there that would unlock the gardening magic others seemed to have in spades. She wanted her plants to thrive in harmony instead of constantly battling against nature. Perhaps this is what you've been wanting: an abundance of vegetables, easy maintenance, and an easier way to garden.

Do you have dreams of overflowing baskets of ripe, juicy tomatoes, fragrant herbs, and flowerbeds buzzing with color? You are not alone in the picture that reality has painted for you: the struggling plants, lackluster yields, and the constant battle against pests. Like our gardener, you follow guides and blogs. You water diligently and give them the most sunlight you can. Yet, your plants just seem... sad. Countless new gardeners hit this wall, and they all feel the same frustration. It also doesn't help when there's contradicting information because it leaves a person not knowing where to even start!

Imagine if there was a solution, though, and not one that involves expensive, harmful chemicals or backbreaking labor. Imagine if you could get that healthy garden by doing something as simple as planting certain plants together. Probably sounds too good to be true, but this is a concept that stretches quite far back in time. This ancient wisdom of companion planting holds the key to unlocking the potential of your garden.

Trust me, I understand the struggles. Starting a garden can be a daunting task. There's the bombardment of endless choices: what plants you should get, how to maximize space, and how to find time to properly tend to the garden with everything else you have to get done in a day. Let's not forget the pests and diseases that have to be kept away. Oh, we can top *that* off with the constant worry about year-round success. That paragraph alone would make someone throw in the towel!

However, let's have some good news. Companion planting addresses all of those concerns in a way that is beginner-friendly, budget-conscious, and good for the environment. Better yet, there is no confusing jargon to decipher, nor will you get lost in the vast sea of information. This book is your friendly guide, tailored to simplify the process and give you the power to make a thriving garden that flourishes the way nature intended.

Still not convinced? Let's see how your gardening woes are solved.

- There is far less confusion or guesswork. My approach focuses on understanding the relationships between plants: which plants thrive together and how they benefit each other. I even bring practical tips on layout, seasonal planting, and comprehensive maintenance routines. Do you want clear and manageable processes? Here they are!

- You'll learn how you can maximize yield, even in small spaces. I offer creative solutions to every potential gardener. No one is left behind on this journey.

- With your new garden setup, you'll be able to balance your time and still have plenty left over for your garden. Time is precious, and companion planting understands that.

- You will be able to avoid those pesky pests and diseases without using harsh chemicals. With companion planting, you can do this with the power of nature. You'll bring in beneficial insects and create natural repellents, all while building a resilient ecosystem.

- You'll be geared up for year-round success. You won't have to be tied down to seasons because you'll have chosen the right plants.

That's only the tip of the iceberg. You'll have a budget-friendly bounty and a beautiful garden design. But why would I give all this knowledge to you?

I have been a dedicated advocate for sustainable and holistic gardening practices. It's been a lifelong passion of mine to connect with nature, and that's led me to combine ancient wisdom with the latest breakthroughs to make ecosystems that can really flourish. My mission for years has been to empower new gardeners to experience the joys of a flourishing garden that not only benefits the environment but also their well-being.

As you move through this journey, remember that you're not alone. With this book as your guide, you have the knowledge and support to make your gardening dreams a reality. So, let's dig in and embrace the beauty of companion planting. Watch as your garden transforms into a vibrant haven full of life. It's time to experience the joy of growing your food, connecting with nature, and feeling a positive impact on yourself and the world – one seed at a time.

Chapter One

Benefits of Companion Planting

Have you been like our struggling gardener, thinking that the magic of your garden lies solely above the soil? Many gardeners do, but the real magic happens below the surface. It's here that a silent partnership thrives, influencing the world of microbes. While we cannot see them, this intricate partnership, sparked by companion planting, unlocks so much potential for your garden.

Again, our struggling gardener yearned for a vibrant plot of land in her backyard, and she would soon find that companion planting held the key. It's not just wisdom passed down for generations either; a recent study published by NCBI revealed that by planting certain crops together, we are greatly benefiting the microbial world in the soil

(Gao & Zhang, 2023). This chapter unveils the secrets and benefits of companion planting, which will soon give you the power to turn your plot of land into a flourishing ecosystem!

Overview of Companion Planting

I know I have mentioned "ancient wisdom," but companion planting has been woven into the tapestry of horticulture for millennia and is now making its resurgence in modern gardens. While we can contribute this renaissance to the organic movement in the 1970s, we should trace it back to its beginnings. This will demonstrate why it's so important now and the key concepts and principles of companion planting.

The Ancient Methods

The concept of companion planting can be traced back over 2,000 years ago when Egyptian farmers intuitively paired plants, discovering a natural process that boosted crop yield while repelling pests. The Greeks and Romans would follow, focusing on their pairings to boost their grape crops for winemaking. Many civilizations around the globe utilized companion planting techniques which became deeply intertwined with religious ceremonies and rituals surrounding the harmonious relationships between humans and nature.

As centuries passed, the medieval Europeans picked up on the practice of using companion planting in their monastic gardens. They carefully selected herbs and vegetables for their unique benefits, giving them a sustainable, harmonious ecosystem.

But it wasn't until the 'Three Sisters' technique of the Native Americans that people truly saw the power of plant partnerships. The

'Three Sisters' method was practiced for centuries by the Iroquois tribe. They would interplant corn, beans, and squash to create this symbiosis. The corn would give a support structure for the vines of the bean plants while the beans brought nitrogen into the soil, which benefited the corn. Then the sprawling squash plants acted as a living mulch, suppressing weed growth while keeping moisture in the ground for all three plants to thrive. This collaboration was a showcase of the profound understanding of maximizing plant interactions for sustainable crops.

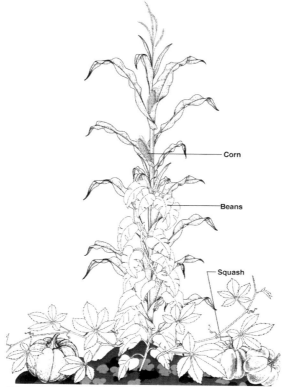

Three Sisters companion plants: corn, beans, and squash.

Relevancy in Today's Gardens

While the roots of companion planting are firmly planted in ancient gardens, it was the organic movement of the 1970s that brought this practice back to the forefront of gardening. The 1970s were a pivotal time due to the growing awareness of the harmful effects of synthetic chemicals, such as pesticides and fertilizers like DDT, which were produced during WWII. These chemicals controlled pests and diseases but also caused great harm to the natural ecosystem and human health. Since the Environmental Protection Agency began banning harmful chemicals, there has been a search for more natural alternatives.

However, the movement was not just about rejecting harmful chemicals. There was also a cultural shift towards achieving interconnectedness with nature, even though something as simple as a garden. Companion planting aligned with these evolving values, leading to the spreading of knowledge and the continued practice of this method. Today, this same approach resonates with our contemporary concerns about ecological balance and sustainable practices.

Key Concepts and Principles

The guiding principle of companion planting is in plant symbiosis. This is when certain plants interact positively, which promotes growth, deters pests, and maximizes efficiency. Plant symbiosis embodies the concept of enduring relationships that can be broken down into two main types: mutualism and allelopathy.

- **Mutualism:** This is the "win-win" scenario or "win-win-win" in the case of the 'Three Sisters' technique, but this is where every plant benefits from the other. It can even be a mutual benefit for helpful insects, like how an acacia tree feeds ant colonies which protects it from herbivores.

- **Allelopathy:** This phenomenon involves the release of chemical compounds by plants that can either benefit or prevent the growth of their neighbors. Having an understanding of allelopathy will allow you to choose the plant combinations that will gain optimal results.

What began as an observation that "these plants just work together" has become a science and an art form of finding the right plant combinations. The advantage of knowing the concepts of companion planting means your garden will get the most benefits.

Benefits of Companion Planting

Beyond its historical charms and cultural significance, companion planting is a natural way to save a gardener time and money by choosing plant partners that can assist each other in achieving bountiful harvests. It's more than recreating the ancient gardens; it's now about creating interactions that create thriving, resilient, and high-yielding gardens. Planting the right combination of plants can save a lot of time because they work in harmony and have many more benefits, so let's look at some of the key benefits you'll get by embracing this concept.

- **Allows for diversity:** Companion planting thrives on diversity. Unlike common monocultures, which are prone to pests and diseases, diverse plant combinations come together to make a mutually beneficial ecosystem. Every plant brings unique qualities, from those that repel pests or boost nutrient levels to the ones that simply provide some structural support. This collection of interactions not only makes your garden healthier but also creates a balanced and sustainable environment where all your plants have an opportunity to flourish.

- **Boosts garden growth:** We turn back to our key principles and concepts as companion planting unleashes the power of plant symbiosis. When certain plants are paired, they will promote each other's development, which means faster growth and increased productivity. Legumes like peas and beans act as natural fertilizers, enriching the soil with nitrogen, which is ideal for something like corn. This example is a call back to the 'Three Sisters' technique, one of the countless partnerships to explore in the garden.

- **Keeps pests away:** Every gardener wants to keep unwanted visitors away, and certain companion plants contain potent deterrents against pests. Something fragrant like basil or garlic unleashes their aroma, deterring pests while protecting plants like tomatoes. The vibrant blooms of a marigold release chemicals that repel nematodes, which are microscopic worms that live in your soil and wreak havoc on plant roots. When you introduce natural deterrents, you create a healthier garden environment, reduce your need for harsh chemicals, and promote a more sustainable approach to pest control.

- **Attracts beneficial pollinators:** A robust and productive garden needs pollinators. Companion planting is a natural and effortless way to attract these beneficial allies into your garden. Vibrant flowers, like marigolds and lavender, attract pollinators, such as butterflies and bees, with an irresistible allure of colorful, fragrant blooms packed with pollen. As these insects feast on flowers, your garden vegetables benefit by increasing the reproduction of fruiting plants leading to a flourishing garden and plentiful harvest at the end of the growing season. It's another win-win scenario.

- **Creates fertile ground:** So, you already have a good idea about one of the ways your soil will benefit from companion planting. When the same type of plant is planted in large crops, like corn, it will suck out certain nutrients from the soil, but when paired with beans, aids in putting nutrients back in, and the neighboring plants benefit. This process entails nitrogen-fixing bacteria in legumes that are continuously released while they grow and when the plant decays. These combinations can benefit overall soil health and nutrient composition for your garden. In other cases, where the soil is compacted, root vegetables like carrots and radishes act like nature's drills to loosen the soil for neighboring plants to spread their roots to grow. Cover crops can also help. Something like clover adds organic matter, prevents erosion, and increases microbial activity, enhancing soil structure, fertility, and water retention.

- **Conserves water:** Companion planting with certain plant combinations creates a nearly self-sustaining microclimate that helps conserve water. Groundcover plants like clover and squash retain moisture by minimizing soil exposure and evaporation from the sun. When paired with taller plants, those tall plants provide shade for their ground companions. This strategy reduces the need for frequent watering, especially in the dry, hot summer months.

- **Suppresses weeds:** This is a great method if you want a natural solution to weed control. Groundcovers act as mulch, so while they're conserving water and eliminating soil erosion, they are also preventing weeds from growing. This saves labor hours when you don't need to manually weed the garden, giving you more time to enjoy it.

- **Provides an alternative to chemicals:** This is one of the biggest reasons companion planting has regained popularity today. When you combine the natural abilities of plants to support each other, you're creating a healthy, productive garden that doesn't need to rely on synthetic fertilizers or pesticides that contain harsh chemicals that are bad for the environment. This also ensures you're getting safe, quality produce and promoting a cycle of beneficial growth.

Embracing Natural Gardening Methods

The appeal of growing your own fresh, homegrown produce is undeniable, but what are some benefits of choosing gardening methods that don't rely on store-bought pesticides or other harmful chemicals? While convenient options are on your grocery shelves, what makes companion planting on your own all worthwhile? Let's look at the five key advantages that you'll get from natural gardening.

- **Extra flavor and nutrients:** By steering clear of artificial fertilizers and pesticides and instead combining plants that enrich soil nutrients, you promote a healthy ecosystem. This vitality will be reflected in the nutrient-rich vegetables on your plate. Research indicates that pesticides can have adverse effects on nutrient absorption and the growth of specific plants. Moreover, pesticides not only impact the soil but also affect sunlight and photosynthesis when they are sprayed onto plants, leaving a thin film (Bondareva, 2021). Employing companion planting techniques to avoid these pesticides can boost your garden's natural ability to repel harmful bugs and diseases, all while preserving the plant's capacity to absorb nutrients from both the soil and the sun.

- **Harvests that are friendly to your wallet:** While there are high costs to set up a productive garden, you can't overlook the long-term savings. All you have to do is think about the cost of organic produce from the grocery store now. Think about the number of trips you *won't* be making to the grocery store, too, because you have what you need in your garden. Every carrot, tomato, and other vegetable is a small victory for your wallet.

- **You impact the future:** Food choices impact the planet. With large-scale farming practices, there is a huge reliance on chemicals, which contribute to water pollution and give off carbon dioxide, contributing to higher levels of greenhouse gasses. Not only does this produce more carbon dioxide, but the deforestation of land areas for large-scale farming massively cuts down the oxygen-producing trees, accelerating the amount of carbon dioxide in the atmosphere. By choosing natural techniques, we are minimizing the environmental footprint. While one person alone can't save the planet, the more people choose harmonious gardening practices, the higher hopes we have of making a significant change to our planet's health.

- **Establishing a deeper connection with nature:** Gardening is much more than growing food. It's about forging a deep bond with the world around you. As you care for your plants, you observe their life cycle miraculously unfold in front of you, making you develop a deeper appreciation for the environment and the source of your food. You'll taste those rewards in endless bites, too. The act of planting, tending, and harvesting turns into a meaningful process. It grounds you in the present moment, which lets you foster a sense of peace and accomplishment. Natural gardening can be a deeply enriching endeavor, contributing to your overall well-being.

- **You'll create a garden teeming with life:** Gardens are ecosystems, buzzing with life. Unlike monoculture farms that use chemicals to control every aspect, gardens attract an array of beneficial insects. You'll be able to look out at your garden and see ladybugs, lacewings, and hoverflies. And while they are controlling your pest population, they add a layer to your garden that's beneficial to the environment. Additionally, when you use composting and cover cropping, you create a haven for beneficial bacteria, earthworms, and fungi. That's so much life in such a small space!

There are numerous benefits and successes on the gardening journey, and there will be moments when you face some challenges. Instead of declaring defeat, remind yourself of the numerous benefits, and that with persistence and resilience, great rewards will outweigh the challenges. So how do you keep your spirits high in the face of unpredictable weather, or sneaky insects breach your defenses. Sometimes, those challenges can feel like so much all at once, but you just need to look back here and remember that the rewards are worth the challenges. So, how do you approach gardening to keep your spirits up when you run into challenges?

Cultivating Success by Setting Realistic Goals

We all yearn to step out into our vibrant green world, our senses awakening to the fragrance of blooming herbs and the industrious sounds of bees. Where many gardeners struggle isn't months into the growing season; it's the obstacles they place in their own path before they even sow their first seed. So, before you grab a garden tool and charge ahead, remember that this adventure begins with a single, realistic step.

One of the initial tasks is to let go of the idea of replicating Pinterest-perfect landscapes. Instead, focus on the excitement of small victories. For you, this might begin with a window box, an upcycled pallet, or even a single pot by your door. Your first foray into gardening should be manageable, a place to experiment, learn from missteps and revel in your initial successes.

Additionally, be prepared for moments of confusion and perhaps frustration. A seedling might refuse to sprout, or you could face a sudden pest invasion. Such challenges are common even for seasoned gardeners but should not be seen as failures. They are opportunities for growth and discovery. Embrace the learning curve, for it is in the journey, not the destination, that the joy of gardening truly lies.

Consider the needs of your plants. Embrace the rhythm of the seasons, preparing seeds and seedlings in late winter and early spring for the warmth to come. This preparation ensures strong roots for the summer months and a bountiful harvest before the first frost. Adapt to the natural ebbs and flows, a topic we will explore further in this book.

Set realistic gardening goals by letting practicality guide you. Which plants appeal to you? Which vegetables are staples in your kitchen? Which plants are visually appealing? Many of these questions will be addressed in the Interactive Element sections of this book. Once you have chosen your preferred plants, explore companion planting to maximize their growth.

Consider your available resources. Water is crucial, so ensure you can provide for your plants' needs. Some plants require frequent watering, while others thrive with less. Additionally, consider nourishment. While companion planting benefits your plants, they still require ample nutrients throughout the growing season.

With realistic goals in mind, let's begin to uncover your dream garden wish list.

Interactive Element: Dream Garden Wish List

1. Top Veggie: *My favorite vegetable that I can't wait to grow is:*

2. Companion Herbs: *Herbs that I love and will complement my top veggie are:*

3. Colorful Veggies: *I'd love to add a pop of colorful veggies like:*

4. Crunchy Delight: *A crunchy vegetable for snacking that I adore is:*

5. Leafy Greens: *A leafy green that I enjoy in salads or as a side dish is:*

6. Unique Twist: *Adding a unique vegetable that intrigues me, such as:*

7. Space-Saver: *Considering a compact or vertical-growing vegetable for limited space, like:*

8. Seasonal Surprise: *A vegetable that thrives in my local climate and brings seasonal delight, such as:*

ele

Now that you are familiar with this ancient wisdom and have an idea of how to approach this realistically, you are ready to get started with a key component of companion planting: planning your garden.

Chapter Two

Abundant Garden Plans

*Divide your garden into blocks, dedicating each block
to specific types of veggies that benefit one another based
on companion planting suggestions. Leave enough space
between each plant to allow for their natural spread.*

Anonymous

In this chapter, we will begin unlocking the doors of companion planting layouts. Think about dividing your garden layout into flourishing spaces, each thriving with complementary veggie groups. Every careful consideration provides its own set of benefits, leaving you with choices that lead you to an abundant garden.

This concept isn't just about making up plant friendships on a whim. The layout will be crucial in getting the maximum benefits of companion planting. When you strategically arrange your garden, you open up a harmonious haven for all your plants. You can think of this as fostering a mutually beneficial community where each veggie plays a role in boosting your garden's overall health and productivity.

There is a lot of information to take in to unlock the secrets of your garden plan, so get ready as I guide you through various strategies, planning techniques, and other growing considerations. This will equip you with the correct tools to create a nearly perfect layout for your veggie cliques.

Essential Conditions for Abundant Gardens

Before you step out into the garden and get your hands dirty, choosing the right location for your garden is essential. You might think, *Yeah, backyard, of course,* but there are other factors to consider when selecting the prime backyard real estate that will contribute to a flourishing garden. So, let's uncover those considerations.

Sunlight Exposure

Sunlight is one of the key elements of your garden. Most veggies require at least six to eight hours of *direct* sunlight daily. There are some, like your leafy greens, that can tolerate partial shade. What this means for you is that you have to consider the sunlight patterns throughout the day.

Does the chosen location get consistent sun, or will trees and other buildings cast shadows? You can sketch a sun map that will track sunlight's movement and help you identify the sunniest patch in your yard. Keep in mind that even a few extra hours of sun each day can significantly help your crops.

Water Accessibility

Refilling and carrying around a watering can multiple times each day can turn strenuous; therefore, your location should have easy access to water. Putting your garden near a spigot or a rainwater catchment system will help tremendously, especially in the hotter months.

Think about your soil, too. How does it manage water or moisture levels? Soil with poor drainage can lead to waterlogged roots and unproductive plants. If you are in an area with soil that doesn't drain well, your soil may have high clay content, and you might consider raised beds for increased control over soil conditions.

Soil Quality

Soil plays a huge role, which is why we will delve deeper into it in Chapter 4. However, it is worth mentioning here because your site should have fertile, well-draining soil. Simple soil tests can let you understand more about the land where your plants will grow. It's important to remember that even average soil can be amended with compost and other organic matter to make the right environment for your plants.

Level Ground or a Gentle Slope

Uneven grounds can lead to harmful erosion and uneven watering. You'll want the site to be level, or you can amend it to be level. A gentle slope can also work in your favor. You can always use the slope as a drainage system, flowing water away from your garden beds. Terracing can also be used to create sloped gardens. This will allow your plants that need more water to thrive at the bottom while preventing soil erosion.

Wind Protection

There's nothing wrong with a gentle breeze. Some wind can actually help strengthen plant stalks as they grow from a seedling, but strong winds can cause significant damage to delicate seedlings and even topple your established plants. Look for a location that's protected from prevailing winds. This could be by a fence, outbuilding, or even hedges. Alternatively, you could use wind-resistant crops (kale and Swiss chard) on the perimeter to act as windbreaks for your more fragile vegetables.

Microclimate Factors

You can't underestimate the subtle influences that can create a microclimate in your garden. A nearby structure like your shed or a wall can create shade and affect heat, creating a space for plants that thrive in cooler, shadier areas.

Consider your local wind patterns, potential pockets of frost, and even the presence of hard surfaces in your yard that will radiate heat.

Having an understanding of these nuances will let you create micro-zones in your garden that you can tailor to grow a wider variety of plants.

Effective Garden Layouts and Strategies

Choosing the right spot for your garden is like choosing the foundation for the home you live in, which means that it has to be just right! But fear not because whether you're just starting or have a serious green thumb, this guide can help you evaluate and select the ideal layout for your garden needs.

- **Beginner:** Starting small is the key! Think about something manageable like a 10x10 ft (100 sq ft) plot that gives you room to expand. You should pick a location that gives you the ideal amount of sunlight (six to eight hours) every day. The area should also be easily accessible from your home, as this makes watering and tending much easier. As you gain confidence, add more sections during the following growing seasons. Also, remember that three to five carefully chosen veggies will give you plenty of harvest during the summer months.

- **Intermediate:** When you are feeling successful with your beginning garden, you can expand it to around 300-500 sq ft. This size of the garden is fairly suitable for a family of four if you follow the generalized idea that 100 sq ft is sufficient for one person. Look for areas that can be incorporated into your existing routine. They don't all have to be next to the original garden. Also, keep in mind that this expansion should still have well-draining soil and protection from strong winds.

- **Advanced:** If you're ready to take things to the next level, increase your garden size to around 200 sq ft per person. This is when you get to fully embrace experimentation; therefore, try different layouts and incorporate more exotic or other challenging vegetables. With bigger gardens comes much more responsibility, so make sure you have the time and the resources to effectively manage a larger space.

- **Small spaces:** Even if you're working with less space, don't worry! Even urban balconies and patios can become thriving gardens. You can maximize your yields by bringing in vertical gardening techniques, which can range from hanging planters and trellises to container planting. A square-foot gardening method, which we will cover later, is perfect when planting multiple crops in a compact area. Your rule of thumb is to make every inch count.

Garden Layout Types

You want your garden to be gorgeous, but we can't think about just aesthetics here. This is about maximizing space, yield, and enjoyment. Knowing your layout options can make all the difference in choosing a garden that will thrive under your care.

- **In-ground gardens:** This is a classic design, perfect for those with much larger spaces and more diverse plant life. Common plants are tomatoes, peppers, squash, and cucumbers, but keep in mind that soil preparation is a must.

- **Block layout:** Block layouts group your crops into neat squares, which is great for companion planting and reducing soil erosion. Block gardens are ideal for carrots, onions, lettuce, and spinach.

- **Traditional rows:** Sometimes you can't go wrong with the classics! These straight rows give easy access and are perfect for those with large gardens. You will create a happy place for corn, beans, peas, and potatoes in this layout.

- **Vertical gardening:** Vertical gardening in small spaces works like a charm. Trellises, hanging baskets, and containers will let you grow things like tomatoes, beans, strawberries, and herbs.

- **Square-foot method:** If you are merely starting or trying to maximize a small space, this method divides your garden into manageable 1x1 ft sections. While there are limitations, you can still enjoy radishes, carrots, lettuce, and herbs in this setup.

- **Raised beds:** These elevated beds will give you amazing drainage, soil control, and weed resistance. They can even help with pest control, too. This is a perfect method for those in limited spaces or working against challenging soil. You will see tomatoes, peppers, herbs, and salad greens flourish in this design.

Keep in mind that the best design for you will depend on your taste, available space, goals, and budget.

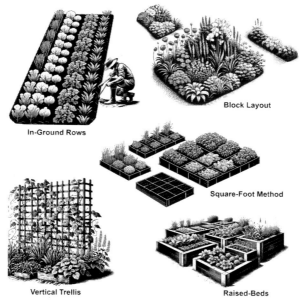

Five types of garden layouts.

Companion Planting Garden Design Principles

Now that we've covered different garden layouts, let's dig into companion planting and garden design. When designing for companion planting, there are several factors to consider, such as your garden size and location. Different strategies will work better in various settings. In this section, we'll explore three popular companion planting designs, discussing their characteristics, potential plant pairings, and suitable layouts.

1: Kitchen Garden

The kitchen garden is often the first choice for beginners, offering a variety of classic edible vegetables for fresh, flavorful meals right from your backyard. To make the most of your kitchen garden, consider companion plants that enhance each other's flavors. Remember the saying, "What tastes good together, grows well together." Mixing vegetables and herbs will not only inspire creative dishes but also help deter pests and diseases, ensuring a bountiful harvest of delicious ingredients.

- **Garden Location:** Backyard setting with a readily accessible water source.

- **Garden Size:** Adaptable, ranging from small raised beds to containers and larger plots.

- **Garden Type:** Raised beds, in-ground beds, or container planting. Dedicate sections for herbs, vegetables, and other edible plants.

- **Sunny or Shady:** Mostly sunny, but some shade is beneficial for heat-sensitive plants.

- **Soil Type:** Well-draining, fertile soil amended with compost or organic matter.

Plant Pairing Examples

- **Tomato with basil:** Basil deters tomato pests while complementing the tomato plant's nutrients.

- **Pepper with chives:** Chives attract beneficial insects that protect pepper plants from pests.

- **Lettuce with nasturtiums:** Nasturtiums act as a trap crop for aphids, protecting lettuce.

- **Cucumber with dill:** Dill attracts pollinators and enhances cucumber flavor.

2: Three Sisters Plus

The three sisters plus garden design combines corn, beans, and squash, utilizing their natural symbiosis. This approach requires ample space, as squash plants spread horizontally and corn grows vertically. Other plant combinations, like sunflowers with zucchini, can mimic this synergy. Sunflowers attract pollinators and shield zucchini from strong winds. Adding pepper plants to this mix can naturally repel aphids from your plants. While the three sisters method offers a traditional approach, experimenting with different plant combinations can lead to exciting discoveries in your garden!

- **Garden Location:** Sunny area with space for vertical growth.

- **Garden Size:** Small plots or dedicated sections within larger gardens.

- **Garden Type:** Raised beds or mounds. Incorporate vertical structures like poles or trellises.

- **Sunny or Shady:** Requires full sun exposure.

- **Soil Type:** Nutrient-rich, well-draining soil amended with compost or organic matter.

Plant Pairing Examples

- **Corn, beans, and squash:** Corn provides climbing support for beans, which replenishes nitrogen for the corn, while squash acts as a living mulch.

- **Sunflowers:** Attract pollinators and deter pests.

- **Marigolds:** Repel various insects while adding vibrancy to your garden.

3: Community Garden

If you're part of a community garden, you can design your companion planting garden to complement your neighbors' plots. Working collaboratively with other gardeners can be rewarding, offering opportunities to learn from each other's experiences and share in the garden's maintenance. Community gardens are typically set in large urban or suburban areas, providing access to shared resources and a sense of community.

- **Garden Location:** Sunny, accessible space that allows shared responsibility and resources.

- **Garden Size:** Varies depending on the community and available space.

- **Garden Type:** All types of designated plots including: in-ground, blocks, and raised beds, or a combination. Individual or shared plots for maintenance.

- **Sunny or Shady:** Mostly sunny, with areas for shade-loving plants.

- **Soil Type:** Well-draining, fertile soil that requires collective maintenance.

Plant Pairing Examples

- **Tomatoes, peppers, and eggplants:** Group plants with similar needs for watering and pest control.

- **Parsley, chives, and basil:** Scatter fragrant herbs throughout the garden to attract beneficial insects.

- **Lettuce, spinach, and kale:** Plant these shade-enjoying plants under taller crops to maximize production.

These are only a few examples; we will dig deeper into more plant pairings later. However, you might want to consider incorporating edible flowers and other pollinator-friendly plants for more diversity and function. A good rule of thumb is to experiment and find what works best in your particular garden.

Plant Selection

Now that you have spent some time pre-planning your garden design and layout, you can select your plants! When creating your dream garden, it's essential to consider how different plants will complement one another for a healthy garden. Keep in mind that not every plant will be suitable for your garden. Some plant pairings might compete for water and nutrients, whereas others might have a strong aroma that can alter the taste and smell of adjacent plants. It's all about creating harmony, so how do you get the optimal ensemble?

The key lies in understanding the unique role each plant plays.

- **Using space efficiently:** Maximize every inch of soil with vertical and horizontal growing power. Towering plants will offer protective shade to your plants below that need some shade or a sturdy structure for climbing plants, and then the sprawling plants fill the gaps. It's about getting the most out of every inch of your garden!

- **Nutrient sharing and provision:** You want to create mutually beneficial exchanges. What plants will benefit from another one? Maybe you need a nitrogen-fixing legume to benefit your tomato plants. Or you could use a leafy green like spinach to provide more shade to the organic matter that will feed your root-growing vegetables.

- **Physical protection and support:** What plants can offer shelter and stability? Going back to the three sisters method, corn not only gives beans a structure to climb, but it shades the squash below. Another example would be taller herbs like rosemary shielding more delicate plants like lettuce from harsh winds.

- **Weed control:** Think about the plants that will weave in and close up the gaps in your soil. You could add low-growing thyme to carpet the ground and add an aromatic charm. There's also potential to use fast-growing radishes to suppress weed growth among slower-maturing beets.

- **Disease control:** Companion planting can be great at enhancing natural resistance. Some plant selections have natural pest and disease resistance, so research your desired plants to create a resilient ecosystem.

- **Insect control:** Make your garden appealing to beneficial insects, and you will have a garden that naturally repels pests. Dill can attract ladybugs that will devour aphids. Hoverflies can come in and feast on the mealybugs attracted to garlic and onions. Those vibrant marigolds that I mentioned? Those are great at deterring harmful beetles, too.

- **Soil improvement:** Companion planting can enrich your soil for long-term health. Deep-rooted plants like borage will bring essential nutrients from the depths up to the surface. Root vegetables keep soil from compacting, and there are plants like nitrogen-fixers, like beans and other legumes, that will put nutrients back into the soil. Think of it as steps in one season that will benefit next year's garden.

- **Speed of growth:** Make sure that your garden is getting balanced development. This will need research into growth rates, but consider these when pairing to avoid any competition. Radishes grow faster than beets, so let them mark the rows. Or plant slower-growing carrots under the shade of taller spinach. This can also be a factor to consider in succession planting, which we will discuss later.

Additional Tips for Plant Selection

- **If it tastes good together, it will grow well together.**
  Sure, basil and tomatoes grow well together, but they also
  repel hornworms. Cucumbers and dill make a tangy combination, but dill will attract beneficial insects that can ward
  off cucumber beetles. While pest control is a great incentive,
  plants come together to create a burst of flavor. Fennel and
  carrots come together as a spicy duo while garlic and onions
  add depth to each other's flavor profiles.

- **Money-saving tip: Start small and only grow what you
  eat.** Gardening is a great way to save on groceries. However,
  less is more. Starting small will let you control costs while
  focusing your time and energy on the plants you'll truly use
  and enjoy. By starting with plants you regularly use in your
  cooking, you save money on seeds and soil, and you ensure a
  sustained gardening experience that fits your tastes.

- **Fun tip: Cluster plants in odd numbers.** Clustering
  plants in threes, fives, or sevens can have a more dynamic makeup than gardens with even groupings. Where even
  numbers can set the stage and provide benefits, odd numbers
  can add a subtle variation and a sense of flow. Think again
  of the three sisters, which shows how odd numbers allow
  plants to fill space naturally, preventing awkward gaps and
  overcrowding.

- **Space-saving tip: Grow your garden vertically.** When
  you have limited space, this is the time to embrace efficiency

and work with vertical gardening. Use stakes, trellises, or hanging baskets to maximize the space you do have. By using a combination of containers, hanging baskets, and trellises, you ignore previous limitations. When you grow up instead of out, you not only save space, but you create the same verdant haven you'd find in a traditional garden.

With careful plant selection and simple tips, you can create a garden that is productive and delicious. And further, you can make it visually appealing and budget-friendly.

Season and Climate Considerations

For every gardener, two important maps will become your best friend, the hardiness zone map and the American Horticulture Society map. The most important of these maps is the hardiness zone map, which divides the country into distinct regions from 1 to 13. Let's break those up and give them a closer look. While we will use the US hardiness zone map, keep in mind that there will be similar maps for each country.

- **Cold (Zones 1-3):** These areas have the harshest winters. Cold-resistant plants are a must here, especially with a limited growing season.

- **Mild (Zones 4-7):** Winters will get a bit milder, which will let you explore a wider variety of vegetables, herbs, and flowers.

- **Warm- can include arid and tropical climates (Zones 8-10):** This is where we have our Goldilocks zones. Winters are warmer, and the growing season is extended. However, you will need to think about heat and the number of scorching days.

- **Tropical (Zones 11-13)** Warmth is almost year-round, and temperatures rarely dip below freezing. This is where you will need to look more at heat and drought-resistant crops.

While our main map discloses the winter temperatures, what do we do about the summer heat? The American Horticultural Society (AHS) devised a system that complements the hardiness map by classifying zones based on days above 86 °F. While not as crucial as knowing colder temperatures, knowing how many hot days you'll face will help you choose heat-resistant plants or implement shading options.

Companion Planting Strategies

This chart is a rough guideline based on the USDA map. Keep the AHS heat zone map, which will help you protect sensitive plants in the hottest months. Again, this is a rough guide, so careful consideration and research will ensure your garden thrives.

Zone	Climate	Plant Pairings	Tips	Garden Layout
Zone 1 and 2	Harsh winters (below -45°F), lower temps in warmer months	Plant *Brassicaceae* family (cabbage, broccoli, kale) paired with peas, beans, or lettuce. Plant peas with carrots or spinach. Plant lettuce with radishes or carrots.	Grow cold-hardy vegetables and root vegetables.	Use a compact layout with raised beds.
Zone 3	Harsh winters (-40°F to 30°F), cool temps in the warm months	Same as zone 1 and 2, but with a longer growing season. Plant radishes with lettuce or peas. Plant Swiss chard with beans or tomatoes, potatoes with peas or beans, and garlic near most vegetables.	Some seeds can be started indoors in the early spring. Cover your most vulnerable plants during the coldest periods.	Use raised beds with frost-resistant planting options.
Zone 4	Cold winters (-30°F to 20°F), moderate temps during growing season	Plant asparagus with tomatoes or lettuce, spinach with strawberries or radishes. Utilize three sisters plus plant cucumbers with corn or beans, and corn with beans and squash.	Start some seeds indoors in early spring. Research and use careful selection to extend your growing season.	Raised beds, three sisters, and container gardens.
Zone 5	Cold winters (-30°F to -20°F), moderate temps during growing season	Plant lettuce with carrots, beets, or radishes. Plant a variety of herbs with most vegetables (basil with tomatoes). Plant summer squash with beans or corn.	More seeds can be started in early spring. Consider cold frames and succession planting, which will extend your growing season.	Raised beds, three sisters, and container gardens.

Zone	Climate	Plant Pairings	Tips	Garden Layout
Zone 6	Cold to moderately cold winters (-10°F to -0°F), slightly warmer than zone 5 during the growing season	Plant broccoli with celery or onions. Three sisters works well, plant winter squash with corn and beans.	Start most seeds indoors during early spring, and you might even consider fall planting on certain crops.	Three sisters, and in-ground planting. Your layout becomes more spacious and diverse, with more warm-season options.
Zone 7	Mild winters (0°F to 10°F), warm growing season with a few hot days	Plant eggplant with peppers, cauliflower with celery or peas, peas with carrots or spinach, and corn with beans and squash.	Seeds can be started indoors in late winter, and consider using container gardening for specific needs.	Spacious layout with lots of warm-season veggies, herbs, and flowers. Vertical gardening methods helps shade the sun.
Zone 8	Mild winters (10°F to 20°F), warm growing season, several hot days	Peppers and onions, okra and marigolds, lots of diversity with warm season choices.	Some seeds can be started outdoors in early spring. Consider extending the growing season with row covers or cold frames.	Same as Zone 7, plenty of garden designs to choose from. Research the number of days above 86°F on the AHS heat zone map.
Zone 9	Mild and temperate (20°F to 30°F), extended warm season, long hot period	Plant eggplant with chives, melons with nasturtiums, melons with corn or beans, collard greens with beets or onions, and beans with corn or potatoes.	Most crops can be directly planted outdoors; however, consider heat-tolerant varieties and drought-resistant methods.	Widest array of options, but consider using shade structures to protect heat-sensitive plants during the summer. Use the AHS heat zone map.
Zones 10 and 11	Subtropical to tropical and warm year-round. The coldest temps range from (30°F to 40°F), but there is an extended hot period	Plant succulents (aloe) with other succulents or herbs and beets with lettuce or spinach. You can plant tropical fruits like papaya and watermelon, but they don't require specific companions, so you can use them anywhere in the garden.	Year-round planting is possible. However, focus should be on heat-loving and humidity-tolerant varieties.	Lush layout, with many options available; consider container gardening for more heat-sensitive plants.

Interactive Element

1. Find Your Growth Zone:

- Find out your garden's secret code! Check out the USDA Plant Hardiness Zone Map, a treasure map for your plants to identify your specific growth zone. If you live outside of the US, consult your country's zone map; some links are listed below.

- https://planthardiness.ars.usda.gov/ (United States)

- http://planthardiness.gc.ca/?m=1 (Canada)

- https://www.plantmaps.com/interactive-united-kingdom -plant-hardiness-zone-map-celsius.php (UK)

1. Locate Your Garden Space:

- Assess your yard or available space to determine the most suitable location for your garden. Your yard is an adventure waiting to happen.

- Consider sunlight exposure (six to eight hours), water accessibility, wind protection, and soil quality.

1. Plan for Size and Conditions:

- Plan the size of your garden based on factors such as the number of people you're feeding and the types of crops you want to grow.

- Consider the specific conditions in your area, such as the length of the growing season and average temperatures.

1. **Sketch Your Garden Layout:**

- Create a simple sketch of your garden area layout.

- Optimize space by grouping plants with similar water and sunlight needs and incorporating companion planting principles.

1. **Identify Your Zone's Plants:**

- Explore plants that thrive in your specific growth zone. Online resources (like the one provided below), local growers, and garden centers will give you in-depth help in choosing your plants.

- https://sowtrueseed.com/search?type=article&q=zone This website will walk you through several plants to grow in your region.

These action steps will prepare you to start your gardening journey with a tailored plan considering your unique climate, space, and preferences.

ele

Planning and organization unlock garden success! Use all these considerations and maps to design the best garden and select the plants that will thrive. But now, we must move on to give an in-depth look at plant pairings and how you can create your thriving haven.

Chapter Three

Plant Partners for Stress-Free, Bountiful Gardens

Two things you should not do is plant around large trees and shrubs. Walnut trees release a chemical into the soil that makes it difficult for other plants to grow. Trees and shrubs compete for nutrients and sunlight. To prevent your garden from suffering, don't plant near trees and shrubs.

Montpelier Agway Farm & Garden

Imagine the thrill of planting your first seeds, thinking of your lush garden that's teeming with life; however, reality has other plans for you. You carefully placed seedlings under the shade of your tallest tree to protect them from the summer heat that the seed packet warned you about, but it's been weeks, and they are withered. Your vegetable patch is a buffet for pests. It can be discouraging, but it's a common startup issue for all gardeners, and that's why it's important to plan beyond the seed packet.

Planting is fun, but it's only one part of the adventure. Your garden needs thoughtful placement. So that's where companion planting comes in, right? Plants benefit from one another, but not everything is a perfect match. So, while that tall tree offers shade, it could put chemicals in the surrounding soil to prevent any competition. Let's not forget that the tree will suck up precious water and nutrients, leaving your plants with nothing.

In this chapter, we will navigate the science behind plant partnerships, discovering what combination works best to unlock a beautiful, resilient, and thriving garden.

Plant Pairing Guide

Your garden is going to thrive on collaboration. Just like we as humans find strength in our community, plants can benefit tremendously from partnering with the right neighbors. You want to use the natural synergies between different species to make a thriving, balanced ecosystem in your garden.

Like humans, not all placements are going to equal a harmonious union. Where some pairings offer mutual benefits, others will turn into competition, stunted growth, or a complete garden failure. When you understand these dynamics, you will make the right choices to benefit everything in your garden.

Beneficial Plant Pairings

- **Living mulch and vegetables:** Leafy groundcovers like clover or lettuce turn into a living mulch. Mulches will help you control weeds, and keep moisture and nutrients in the soil. It's a great environment for tomatoes, peppers, and eggplants.

- **Nitrogen fixers and heavy feeders:** Legumes like beans and peas convert atmospheric nitrogen and release it into the soil, called nitrogen fixation. This process creates a soil perfect for plants to soak up a lot of nutrients: heavy feeders like corn, pumpkins, and sunflowers. This relationship will reduce your need for fertilizers like compost.

- **Trap crops and pest deterrents:** Strong-smelling plants like mint, marigolds, and chives will repel harmful insects while protecting neighboring vegetables. They also work by attracting beneficial pollinators. Nasturtiums, for example, act as "trap crops" by attracting aphids away from your more valuable plants.

- **Pollinators and food sources:** Flowering herbs and companion plants like borage, dill, and vibrant flowers will attract bees and butterflies. These pollinators are essential for the production of fruits and vegetables.

Why These Pairings Work

These beneficial pairings work because they exploit natural synergies, which creates a balanced environment. Living mulch will suppress weeds while providing nutrients, nitrogen fixers enrich the soil for heavy feeders, and pest deterrents give natural protection. By having carefully planned pairings, you will find that your garden houses healthier plants, reduced pest problems, and increased yields.

Unfriendly Neighbors

- **Heavy feeders and nutrient depleters:** Planting heavy feeders like corn next to shallow-rooted vegetables like lettuce can lead to competition between your plants for water and nutrients. This power struggle will lead to the stunted growth of the weaker plant.

- **Allelopathic plants:** Unlike nitrogen fixers, some plants release chemicals into the nearby soil deterring the growth of other sensitive vegetables or flowers. This is why you want to avoid planting certain vegetables or any sensitive flowers in the area around the plants that give off these types of chemicals.

- **Same family, same problems:** Planting vegetables from the same family together does run the risk of attracting pests and diseases. It is commonly seen with tomatoes, peppers, and eggplants (nightshades). It can also happen if you plant tomatoes one year and eggplants the next year. Therefore, separating plants of the same family has a better chance of warding off pests. This also makes it important to practice crop rotation.

- **Climbing vines and fragile plants:** Climbing vines like clematis or morning glories can engulf more delicate plants like flowers and herbs. It will smother and shade them, causing stunted growth, poor flowering, or even death.

Why These Pairings Should Be Avoided

These pairings will disrupt any balance you have achieved in your garden ecosystem. Heavy feeders will bully weaker plants, allelopathic plants have the potential to make toxic zones, and you'll host pests and diseases by planting the same family together or not rotating your crops. You also don't want a climbing vine engulfing and wiping out your more delicate plants.

Vegetable Companion Planting Chart

For this chart, we will look at some of the most common additions to a garden. You'll also get to see ideal companion plants for each of them, their foes, the plants that will detract pests, and which plants will attract friendly pollinators.

Garden Crop	Companion Plants	Adversary Plants	Pest Detractor	Pollinator Attractor
Asparagus	basil, beets, eggplant, lettuce, spinach, strawberries, tomatoes, other nightshades	carrots, garlic, onions, potatoes	nasturtium, petunias	borage, dill
Basil	beets, chives, garlic, peppers, purslane, tomatoes, other nightshades	cucumber, fennel, rue, sage, thyme	marigolds, nasturtium, oregano	borage, lavender
Beans	three sisters (beans, corn, and squash) broccoli, cabbage, carrots, cauliflower, cucumbers, eggplant, garden peas, potatoes, radishes, strawberries, tomatoes	asparagus, beets, fennel, garlic, kohlrabi, onion, sunflowers, other alliums	nasturtium, dill	borage, lavender, marigolds
Beets	allium family, broccoli, cauliflower, cabbage, garlic, lettuce, radishes	chard, field mustard, pole beans, spinach	dill, hyssop	borage, nasturtium
Broccoli	beets, Brussels sprouts, cabbage, cauliflower, celery, oregano, potatoes, radishes, spinach	corn, eggplant, lima beans, onions, squash, strawberries, tomatoes	dill, nasturtium, rosemary	borage, chamomile, marigolds
Brussels sprouts	arugula, basil, beans, beets, carrots, garlic, mint, nasturtium, peas, radishes, spinach, thyme	fennel, pole beans, onions, strawberries, tomatoes, zucchini	chamomile, dill, nasturtium	marigolds

Garden Crop	Companion Plants	Adversary Plants	Pest Detractor	Pollinator Attractor
Cabbage	basil, beets, broccoli, Brussels sprouts, cauliflower, celery, collard greens, kale, kohlrabi, potatoes	lettuce, rue, strawberries, tomatoes	dill, nasturtium, rosemary	borage, marigolds, yarrow
Carrots	beans, chives, lettuce, onions, peas, radish, tomatoes, thyme	dill, celery, corn, fennel, leeks, lettuce, parsnips, potatoes, winter squash, zucchini	nasturtium	borage, lavender, marigolds
Cauliflower	beets, Brussels sprouts, carrots, celery, corn, garlic, lettuce, peas, potatoes, radish, spinach, Swiss chard	corn, cucumber, mustard, onions, peppers, pumpkins, strawberries, tomatoes, turnips	dill, nasturtium	borage, marigolds
Corn	three sisters (corn, squash, and beans) cucumber, garden peas, melons, potatoes	asparagus *Brassicaceae* family, eggplant, fennel, tomatoes	dill, nasturtium	borage, marigolds
Cucamelon	basil, beans, chives, corn, lettuce, peas, radish, sunflowers	cucumbers, melons, potatoes, squash	calendula, nasturtium	dill, marigolds
Cucumber	beans, beets, celery, corn, kale, peas, radish, sunflowers	basil, fennel, melons, mint, potatoes, pumpkins, sage, zucchini	dill, nasturtium	borage, marigolds
Dill	asparagus, broccoli, Brussels sprouts, cabbage, corn, cucumber, lettuce, onion	carrots, fennel, lavender, tomatoes	nasturtium	borage, marigolds, yarrow

Garden Crop	Companion Plants	Adversary Plants	Pest Detractor	Pollinator Attractor
Eggplant	bush beans, cucumber, lettuce, peas, peppers, radish, spinach	corn, fennel, geraniums, lentils, pole beans, potatoes, zucchini	nasturtium, thyme	borage, marigolds
Garlic	beets, carrots, broccoli, cabbage, cauliflower, eggplant, peppers, spinach, tomatoes, potatoes	asparagus, beans, parsley, sage, other alliums	dill, nasturtium	borage, lavender, roses
Kale	beets, celery, chives, cucumber, garlic, leek, mint, peas, peppers, potatoes, rosemary, sage, spinach	asparagus, beans, broccoli, fennel, onions, strawberries, sunflowers, tomatoes	dill, nasturtium	borage, lavender, marigolds, sweet alyssum
Lettuce	asparagus, basil, beans, beets, carrots, chives, garlic, onions, parsnips, peas, radish, squash, watermelon	*Brassicaceae* family, celery, fennel, foxglove, parsley, sunflowers, tomatoes	chervil, dill, nasturtium, thyme	borage, marigolds, sweet alyssum
Onions	beets, carrots, lettuce, spinach, strawberries, tomatoes	asparagus, beans, *Brassicaceae* family peas, sage, other alliums	dill, nasturtium	borage, lavender, marigolds
Peas	beans, beets, carrots, corn, cucumbers, eggplant, lettuce, peppers, radish, spinach, turnips	chives, garlic, leeks, onions, scallions, shallots	dill, nasturtium, sweet alyssum	borage, lavender
Peppers	basil, carrots, cilantro, onions, oregano, spinach	beans, *Brassicaceae* family, fennel, potatoes	marigolds, marjoram, nasturtium	borage, lavender

Garden Crop	Companion Plants	Adversary Plants	Pest Detractor	Pollinator Attractor
Potatoes	beans, broccoli, cabbage, cauliflower, corn, lettuce, peas	asparagus, cucumbers, eggplant, fennel, okra, peppers, squash, sunflower, tomatoes	calendula, horseradish, nasturtium, tansy	borage, lavender
Radishes	beans, carrots, chervil, cucumber, leeks lettuce, onions, oregano, peas, spinach, tomatoes	cauliflower, dill, mustard, potatoes, strawberries, turnip	calendula, nasturtium	borage, marigolds
Rhubarb	asparagus, beans, beets, *Brassicaceae* family, chives, garlic, onions, sage, strawberries	corn, cucumbers, fennel, melons, pumpkins, sunflowers, tomatoes	catnip, marigolds	borage, nasturtium, yarrow
Rosemary	beans, *Brassicaceae* family, carrots, kale, sage, spinach	basil, cucumbers, fennel, mint, pumpkins, tomatoes	chives, garlic	borage, lavender
Spinach	beans, *Brassicaceae* family, carrots, cilantro, eggplant, lettuce, onion, oregano, peas, radish, rosemary, strawberries	beets, corn, dill, fennel, melons, potatoes, squash, Swiss chard, sunflowers	cosmos, nasturtium, zinnias	borage, marigolds, sweet alyssum
Squash (winter and pumpkins)	three sisters (squash, corn, and beans), lettuce, oregano, peas, radishes	*Brassicaceae* family, carrots, potatoes	buckwheat, calendula, dill, nasturtium	borage, marigolds, sunflowers

Garden Crop	Companion Plants	Adversary Plants	Pest Detractor	Pollinator Attractor
Strawberries	allium family, asparagus, bush beans, caraway, chives, lettuce, rhubarb, spinach	coriander, cucumber, eggplants, mint, okra, peppers, potatoes, squash, tomatoes	catnip, dill, garlic, sage	borage, lavender, thyme, yarrow
Sunflowers	allium family, cucumber, garlic, peppers, pumpkins, tomatoes, winter squash, zucchini	hyssop, fennel, pole beans, potatoes	basil, chives	clover, daisies, marigolds
Tomatoes	asparagus, basil, carrots, chives, garlic, onions, parsley, radish, squash, thyme	*Brassicaceae* family, corn, dill, fennel, nightshade family, melons, peas, potatoes, rosemary	calendula, nasturtium	borage, cilantro, lavender, marigolds, oregano, sunflowers
Watermelon (and other melons)	beans, carrots, chives, corn (plant corn so it won't block the sun), garlic, leeks, lettuce, okra, peas, radishes	cucumber, mint, potatoes, pumpkins, squash, sunflowers, tomatoes, zucchini	chamomile	lavender, marigolds, nasturtium
Zucchini	three sisters (zucchini, corn, and beans) garlic, lettuce, peas, radish	*Brassicaceae* family, cucumbers, kohlrabi, potatoes, pumpkins, melons	buckwheat, dill, marigolds, nasturtium, sunflowers	chamomile, lavender, oregano, zinnias

Easiest Plants to Grow

For this section, we will look at 9 vegetables, 5 herbs, and 5 flowers that are the easiest to grow in multiple zones. These are great for beginning gardeners and for anyone looking to have more success with their first companion garden.

For each of these plants, we will look at their companions, their adversaries, their ideal zones, and the reason why they work for your garden. Keep in mind that subzones and your specific climate may affect how things grow. Also, remember to check country-specific zone maps if you find yourself outside the United States.

Top Nine Easy to Grow Vegetables

Radishes

- **Companions:** lettuce, spinach, beans, nasturtiums, marigolds, chervil, peas

- **Adversaries:** *Brassicaceae* family, potatoes, and strawberries

- **Ideal zone:** 3-9

- **Why:** Radishes mature quickly and won't compete for space. Their companions are effective at attracting pollinators and deterring pests. Radishes belong to the same family as cauliflower and broccoli, known as the *Brassicaceae* family, and they will compete for nutrients. Avoid potatoes and strawberries because they share similar plant diseases.

Lettuce

- **Companions:** radishes, carrots, onion, beets, chives

- **Adversaries:** tomatoes, peppers, eggplant

- **Ideal zone:** 3-9

- **Why:** Lettuce is an early and fast grower, and it won't compete for space. It thrives in cooler weather and in partial shade. The companion plants, like root vegetables, deter pests, and they add nutrients to the soil. Avoid planting near sun-loving plants and nightshades (plant adversaries) because they will compete for nutrients and stunt lettuce growth.

Green Beans

- **Companions:** corn, potatoes, tomatoes, strawberries, marigolds

- **Adversaries:** onions and garlic

- **Ideal zone:** 3-9

- **Why:** Beans are one of the plants that fix nitrogen in the soil, which benefits other plants (three sisters). Companion plants will deter pests while attracting pollinators. Avoid onions and garlic, as these will slow bean growth because they will compete for resources.

Zucchini

- **Companions:** beans, corn, marigolds, nasturtiums

- **Adversaries:** potatoes, pumpkins

- **Ideal zone:** 3-10

- **Why:** Zucchini is a fast-growing, productive vegetable. Its companion plants will help with nutrient exchange (nitrogen fixing), like beans, and will also deter pests and attract pollinators. Avoid other planting near other spreaders, like potatoes and pumpkins, because they compete for both space and nutrients.

Cucumber

- **Companions:** beans, corn, peas, marigolds, dill

- **Adversaries:** fennel, potatoes, mint, pumpkins

- **Ideal zone:** 4-10

- **Why:** While cucumbers need consistent moisture and trellising, they are extremely productive plants. Companion plants help fix nitrogen and exchange other nutrients. Avoid fennel, because it secretes chemicals into the soil that can harm the cucumber. Avoid potatoes, mint, and pumpkins as these will compete with your cucumbers for nutrients.

Carrots

- **Companions:** onions, lettuce, tomatoes, dill, thyme

- **Adversaries:** fennel, celery

- **Ideal zone:** 3-7

- **Why:** Carrots are great root vegetables for cooler regions. Harvesting after the first frost makes carrots taste sweeter. Plant them near their companions to break up and improve soil health. Plant partners will deter pests. Avoid planting near fennel and celery, however, because they release chemicals that inhibit carrot growth.

Eggplant

- **Companions:** peppers, beans, marigolds, nasturtiums

- **Adversaries:** potatoes and tomatoes

- **Ideal zone:** 5-12 (can even extend to zone 4)

- **Why:** For those in the warmer regions, eggplants will thrive as long as they are protected from pests. Those pest deterrents will come from your companion plants, and they will attract pollinators. Eggplant, tomatoes, and potatoes all belong to the nightshade family. Avoid planting next to each other as they share similar diseases, and they will compete for resources.

Cherry Tomatoes

- **Companions:** basil, marigolds, nasturtiums, carrots

- **Adversaries:** potatoes, corn, fennel

- **Ideal zone:** 2-11

- **Why:** You will need to use supports, like tomato cages or stakes and twine, but cherry tomatoes are great for space-saving with how compact they are. Their companion plants deter pests, attract pollinators, and improve soil health. Avoid your adversaries because they will compete for resources, and they release chemicals into the soil that inhibit tomato growth.

Cucamelon

- **Companions:** corn, beans, peas, marigolds

- **Adversaries:** cucumber, melons, potatoes, squash

- **Ideal zone:** 5-9

- **Why:** Cucamelons look like tiny watermelons but taste more like a sour cucumber. Also, like cucumbers, they are plants that spread and grow quite rapidly, and they require trellising. Companion plants, like beans and peas, fix nitrogen, and marigolds deter pests, and attract pollinators. Their adversaries compete for resources and share similar diseases.

Top Five Easy-to-Grow Herbs

Mint

- **Companions:** oregano, parsley, tomatoes, marigolds

- **Adversaries:** basil, rue, sage, other mints

- **Ideal zone:** 4-9

- **Why:** Mint is an aggressive plant and will spread quickly. Its companions, though, can tolerate the growth, and tomatoes love mint's pest-repelling properties. Marigolds will deter harmful insects. Adversaries should be avoided as they will inhibit each other's growth.

Thyme

- **Companions:** rosemary, oregano, lavender, cabbage, broccoli

- **Adversaries:** none that are significant

- **Ideal zone:** 5-9

- **Why:** Thyme thrives in sunny regions and with well-draining soil. It is a very universal herbal companion that has no notable adversaries. It is a great ground cover that can help smother weeds, deter pests, and attracts a wide variety of pollinators due to its fragrant scent.

Chives

- **Companions:** carrots, tomatoes, lettuce, marigolds, nasturtiums

- **Adversaries:** none that are significant

- **Ideal zone:** 3-9

- **Why:** Chives are a perennial herb that are part of the allium family, like onions. Their purple flowers attract beneficial insects while repelling some pests. Like thyme, chives are universal, and they can grow like weeds.

Lemon Balm

- **Companions:** most vegetables and herbs

- **Adversaries:** rue, basil

- **Ideal zone:** 4-9

- **Why:** Lemon balm is one of the easiest herbs to grow in the garden. It has a delightful fragrance that attracts pollinators, and is a natural pest deterrent, that poses virtually no threat to its companions. You can harvest lemon balm multiple times, and they are very resilient, springing back to life even after harsh winters. You do want to avoid rue and basil, as they can inhibit each other's growth.

Sage

- **Companions:** rosemary, oregano, lavender, carrots, broccoli

- **Adversaries:** rue, basil

- **Ideal zone:** 5-9

- **Why:** Sage loves well-drained soil and full sunlight, much like its companion plants. However, sage and its companions will not compete for resources. Avoid planting with rue and basil, as they will compete and inhibit each other's growth.

Top Five Easy-to-Grow Flowers

Flowers are more than just color and beauty for your garden. As companion plants, their fragrance and pollen attract beneficial insects, they provide food for pollinators, and some flowers can even deter pests. In this section, each flower notes their top companions and which plants to avoid (adversaries), and if it is native to the United States. While you can grow many types of flowers depending on your hardiness zone, it's important to research and prioritize native plants in your specific region whenever possible, as native plants are beneficial to your local ecosystem and support native pollinators. Non-native plants can become invasive and harm the overall diversity and health of the natural environment, and they can take over any garden competing for nutrients. The list also notes if a flower is edible and what parts of it are, but do be cautious that you are identifying your flowers correctly and making sure they are safe to eat beforehand.

Sunflower

- **Companions:** beans, corn, cucumbers, melons, nasturtiums

- **Adversaries:** hyssop, fennel, potatoes

- **Native:** yes

- **Ideal zone:** 2-11 (different species will exist)

- **Why:** Sunflowers attract pollinators and give shade to other plants. They also have allelopathic properties, which suppress weeds. Adversaries compete for nutrients and sunflowers are toxic to potatoes.

- **Edible:** yes (seeds)

Nasturtium

- **Companions:** tomatoes, squash, beans, herbs

- **Adversaries:** none

- **Native:** no (native to South America)

- **Ideal zone:** 9-11

- **Why:** These plants are a great trap crop for aphids, keeping them away from other plants.

- **Edible:** yes (flowers, leaves, and seeds)

Marigolds

- **Companions:** tomatoes, peppers, eggplant, beans, lettuce

- **Adversaries:** none

- **Native:** no (native to Mexico)

- **Ideal zone:** 2-11

- **Why:** One of the most universal companion flowers for your garden. They attract beneficial insects and deter harmful ones, like nematodes and whiteflies.

- **Edible:** no

Borage

- **Companions:** strawberries, tomatoes, squash, beans

- **Adversaries:** none

- **Native:** no (native to the Mediterranean region)

- **Ideal zone:** 4-8

- **Why:** Borage is drought tolerant, blue flowering herb. It improves the health and flavor of tomatoes and strawberries. Use it to shelter beneficial bugs and attract pollinators.

- **Edible:** yes (flowers and leaves)

Sweet Alyssum

- **Companions:** tomatoes, peppers, cabbage, broccoli, carrots

- **Adversaries:** none

- **Native:** no (native to the Mediterranean region)

- **Ideal zone:** 3-10

- **Why:** This fragrant flower can be used as a ground cover, that attracts beneficial insects while also repelling some pests.

- **Edible:** no

Additional Tips

One thing you can do during your gardening journey is write out a table like the one above. Choose your plants and write them in the first column, then fill out the list of ideal companions, adversaries, and other positives and negatives. This is the best way to make a chart that's suitable not just for your region but for your specific garden.

The following are some other helpful tips.

- **Time-saving tip:** Again, group plants with similar needs for sunlight and water. It simplifies your watering schedule and ensures that all plants thrive.

- **Money-saving tip:** Opt for bare-root plants. These often cost less than potted varieties, and they take to your garden easier with the proper care.

- **Get double-duty plants:** Use vertically growing plants as a natural trellis for your climbing vegetables. It saves space and resources.

- **Check if your flowers are edible:** We did cover some of the best flowers, but remember to look for native plants first. Then, check if they are edible. Not only do they deter pests and add vibrancy to the garden, but they make delicious additions to your dishes.

Interactive Element: Garden Planner

Getting Started

To get started with your garden planner, you need to do the following:

1. Identify your hardiness zone. Remember to find your country's map if you're outside the US (links were provided in Chapter 2).

2. Research the plants listed so far in this book and see what falls within your zone. Consider your favorites, and choose their corresponding companions. Make sure to avoid their adversaries.

3. Remember to start small. Three to five plants will get you started with companion planting, and it will be much easier to manage and ensure success.

4. Look back at your garden design to get a better visualization of plant placement. Remember this will be based on sun-

light, size, and companion planting recommendations.

While many planners will give you freedom when filling them out, some basic tips will help make your planner as effective as it can be.

- **Plant list:** When you choose your plants, you should also list their sun and water needs, spacing requirements, and any helpful tips that you can find about your plant. Look at this carefully, as it will affect your plant placement.

- **Planting schedule:** Plan your sowing and transplanting dates based on your hardiness zone and when your desired harvest time. It will allow you to stagger what you plant for an extended growing season.

- **Companion planting chart:** Again, there are plenty of ideas here about companion plants, but you need to list the companions suitable for your garden.

- **Layout sketch:** Using your planner and the layout sketch, you will be able to come up with plant placements and designated areas.

Printable Garden Planners

While I'm including a couple of different printable versions here, you might find digital planners that offer interactive elements, or you could write out your own. The important aspect is you choose a method that works best for you and your plants.

https://www.myfrugalhome.com/printable-garden-planner/
https://www.therusticelk.com/free-garden-planning-printable/
https://fluxingwell.com/online-free-garden-planner/

Again, everything in this chapter is aimed at helping you get the most out of your companion garden. But what works for one region won't work for another, and what works for you and your garden might not be what works for your neighbor's garden.

Now that you have a rough idea about what your garden will look like, what you're going to grow, and where you'll place it, we can get out there and start getting your garden ready.

Chapter Four

The Gardener's Toolbox and Garden Preparation

According to Gao and Zhang (2023), in the article, *Influence of Companion Planting on Microbial Compositions and Their Symbiotic Network in Pepper Continuous Cropping Soil*, research indicates that companion planting can enhance soil fertility, improve soil enzyme activities, and enrich the diversity of microbial species, ultimately contributing to a healthier soil ecosystem.

The excitement is likely building. You've envisioned your garden with the plants you want and meticulously planned the companion plants that will go with them. All you have to do is get out there and plant, right? We are almost there, and this chapter will serve as the blueprint, guiding you through the initial steps of turning your barren field into a flourishing haven.

Think of your garden as if it were a blank canvas that was waiting for your artistic strokes. Just like any painter out there, you need the right tools, like your trusted trowel and watering can, these will become the key components of your success. Don't be fooled by the surface! The true magic unfolds beneath your feet in the fertile heart of your soil. This is where you will unlock the full potential of companion planting. By nurturing healthy soil with microscopic life, you are laying the foundation for a thriving garden where the benefits of companion planting truly flourish. After knowing what tools you'll need, we will start the most important work with soil preparation. Our navigation through this will empower you to create a nurturing garden for all your plants to thrive.

This chapter will equip you with the fundamental knowledge and techniques to prepare your garden beds. But before we start getting our hands dirty, let's make sure you have the right tools for the job.

Garden Tools and Equipment

Gardening can both be rewarding and daunting at the same time. On one hand, there's excitement in witnessing your garden grow from seedling to harvest, and yet, on the other hand, the choices and tasks can be overwhelming. Luckily having the right tools within reach will make all the difference, allowing you to work comfortably and efficiently. In this section, we will take a look at 13 essential tools and some tips for choosing the right ones for you.

- **Hand trowel:** This may be the most basic, yet essential tool in the gardener's toolkit. While it is small, it is versatile and very affordable. A trowel is great for digging small holes, planting seeds, or transplanting seedlings. You want to choose one that has a comfortable grip and a sturdy stainless-steel blade that won't bend during use. For optimal control, look for a trowel length between 10–12 inches.

- **Pruning shears:** Another essential garden tool. It is also small and affordable. You can shape and control the growth of your plants, and you can easily harvest herbs and vegetables with pruning shears. You will need a couple of options on hand: Bypass pruners for live stems and anvil pruners for dead or woody stems. You want to find sharp, rust-resistant blades that have a clean bypass. The handles should also be comfortable in your hands.

- **Gloves:** Gloves will be your best friend in the garden. They protect your hands from dirt, thorns, and painful blisters. Look for breathable and water-resistant materials like cotton canvas with a nitrile coating, which will have dexterity and puncture resistance. You might also consider features like padded palms, which will give you added comfort for hours spent outside.

- **Hat:** A wide-brimmed hat will offer you protection from the sun while you're in your garden. Materials like straw or cotton are breathable, which allows air circulation, keeping you cool. The brim size should be at least three inches for adequate protection.

- **Hoe:** This tool is one of your workhorses and will be used for weed removal, breaking up soil, and making furrows for planting. You should choose a hoe with a sturdy blade (typically forged carbon steel) and a handle with a comfortable weight and height (varies by person). The type of hoe you need will be based on your needs. Stirrup hoes will let you do shallow weeding, scuffle hoes are great for breaking up soil, and blade hoes are ideal for heavy-duty jobs.

- **Hand cultivator:** This tool helps loosen compacted soil, remove weeds, and aerate garden beds. You'll typically find cultivators with three to five stainless steel tines that are set in place. Some designs can adjust to different angles, too. You want to find a comfortable grip that lets you easily maneuver the tool and keeps you from straining your hands.

- **Garden knife:** A sharp garden knife is also versatile, as it takes on tasks like cutting twine, harvesting vegetables, and pruning small stems. Find a knife with a stainless-steel blade with a comfortable handle. A helpful consideration is to find one with a secure sheath that allows safe storage.

- **Spading fork:** This helps turn your compost, breaks up tough soil, or aerates large areas. You should look for a fork with four to five tines made from forged steel. You also want to look for a long (around four feet, will vary on your height), comfortable handle.

- **Bow rake:** A bow rake will help you gather leaves and debris and can smooth your soil surface. Choose a lightweight rake with a sturdy metal head. The tines should be made of strong, flexible materials like spring steel. Again, you want a handle that is at a comfortable height to prevent back strain. You should maintain an upright posture while using this tool.

- **Loppers:** You can reach and eliminate thicker branches or woody stems that you can't do with pruning shears. You will only need this tool if you plan on using plants with larger woody branches (berry bushes, hedges, shrubs, and trees); otherwise, pruning shears are adequate for most gardeners' needs. Your loppers will have sharp bypass blades made of high-carbon steel. This will allow you to have clean cuts. Your loppers should have comfortable handles and should be the appropriate length for your needs. They will typically be between 18-42 inches.

- **Garden hose:** You can water all your plants with efficiency and effectiveness with a quality garden hose. Look for a heavy-duty hose made from kink-resistant material that is safe for drinking made from polyurethane (rather than polyvinyl chloride or PVC), and labeled "drinking water safe". Ensure that you get a length that reaches all areas of your garden. Also, consider your couplings. Brass or stainless steel are durable and less likely to leak.

- **Watering can:** This tool comes in handy for targeted watering of fragile seedlings, container plants, and any areas that need gentle watering. Choose a can with a comfortable handle for easy carrying. You also want one with a long spout to reach under foliage with an attachment for gentle showering. Choose a watering can between one to two gallons, anything larger can be hard to carry, and it depends on your garden size and plant watering needs.

- **Wheelbarrow:** Make jobs like hauling soil, compost, mulch, or garden debris effortless with a wheelbarrow. You want a sturdy wheelbarrow with a galvanized steel tray for durability and puncture resistance. Consider finding one with comfortable grips and a single large wheel or pneumatic tires that will give you better maneuverability on various terrains. Also, think about the size and weight capacity based on your needs and what you plan to haul.

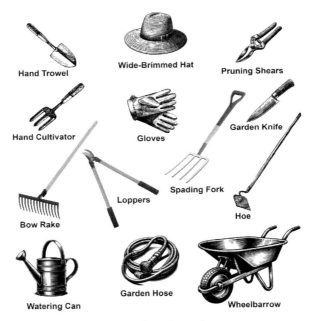

Essential garden tools.

When choosing tools for your gardening endeavors, there are some tips for choosing a quality tool.

- **Material:** Consider durable materials like stainless steel for blades and rust-resistant metals or fiberglass for its handles.

- **Comfort:** Ensure the tools fit your hand size and height. They should let you have a comfortable grip to prevent fatigue and strain.

- **Weight:** Expanding on the previous points, the weight of the tool is important. Wood and steel tend to be heavier than aluminum, plastic, or fiberglass. Select tools with a weight that feels comfortable for you. This helps prevent strain or injury while you're working in your garden.

- **Brand Reputation:** Look at reputable brands known for quality and durability. You want something that will last you several growing seasons. Investing in a better quality tool at a slightly higher price will be worth it.

Cost-Saving Tips

- **Special offers:** Look for deals and promotions on gardening supplies. You'll find many things on sale during the off-season.

- **Used tools:** Borrow or buy used tools instead of choosing something new, especially with the equipment you'll use least.

Fun Tip

- **Tool swap:** Organize a tool swap with your neighbors or a lending library where you can share tools. This can be a fun springtime activity at the beginning of the gardening season.

Preparing the Soil: Things to Know

We have discussed this briefly, but let's dig deeper because you may come across various soil types on your journey. They all possess unique characteristics that will impact plant growth, and they will require specific approaches to achieve optimal results. Here are different soil types that you may find.

Sandy soil: Think about grabbing a handful of sand off the beach—that's the texture you'll get. This soil is composed of large, coarse particles, which allows it to drain exceptionally well. However, that means that it struggles to retain any moisture and nutrients. While it is warm and easy to work with, you will have to frequently water the soil and make amendments with organic matter to have a successful garden.

Clay soil: The texture of clay soil closely resembles molding clay, as it is densely packed with fine particles. This composition allows it to retain water excessively and results in very poor drainage. Clay soil poses challenges for planting, as it can drown plants when wet and tends to harden and compact when dry. Improving drainage and aeration requires amending the soil and employing various gardening techniques.

Silt soil: Silt is like working with flour as it is fine and smooth. Made up of medium-sized particles, it gives you a nice balance of drainage and water retention. This soil is usually fertile and fairly easy to work with, making it a good choice for various plants.

Loam soil: This soil type is a gardener's dream, as it's the perfect blend of sand, silt, and clay in equal proportions. This combination gives excellent drainage and aeration, and it is great at holding onto nutrients. This soil is suitable for a broader array of plants compared to silt.

Peat soil: This spongy, dark soil is rich in organic matter, and it's excellent for retaining moisture. However, it can be acidic and low in essential nutrients. You can amend it with sand or compost to improve drainage and fertility when using peaty soil.

So, how do you know what is the best soil for your garden? Of course, loam soil is a dream for growing lots of plants, but the best soil out there will depend on a few factors.

Climate: In wet regions, such as areas with high rainfall or frequent irrigation, sandy soil is preferred due to its excellent drainage capabilities. Sandy soil allows excess water to pass through quickly, preventing waterlogging and providing better aeration for plant roots. On the other hand, in arid regions with low rainfall and high evaporation rates, clay soil is beneficial for its ability to retain water. The dense structure of clay soil helps to trap and hold moisture, making it available to plants during dry periods. However, clay soil can become hard and compacted, limiting root growth and water infiltration. In such regions, it's important to amend clay soil with organic matter to improve its structure and promote better drainage. Additionally, incorporating mulch and using raised beds can help conserve moisture in sandy soil, while regular cultivation and adding gypsum can improve clay soil's drainage.

Plant preference: Plants have specific soil preferences based on their natural habitat and evolutionary adaptations. Blueberries, for instance, thrive in acidic, peaty soil that is rich in organic matter. This type of soil mimics the conditions found in their native habitats, such as bogs and acidic forests. Blueberries have shallow roots and are sensitive to drought, so the moisture-retentive properties of peaty soil are ideal for their growth. On the other hand, cacti are adapted to arid environments and require well-draining soil to prevent their roots from sitting in water, which can cause rot. Sandy soil provides excellent drainage, allowing excess water to flow away from the roots and preventing waterlogging. This type of soil also warms up quickly, which is beneficial for cacti as they prefer warm soil conditions. Understanding the soil preferences of different plants is crucial for successful gardening. It allows you to provide the optimal growing conditions for each plant, ensuring they thrive and produce healthy foliage or fruits.

Your willingness to amend: Amending soil involves improving its quality by adding materials like compost, manure, or lime to enhance fertility, structure, and drainage. It requires dedication and effort, tailored to the specific needs of your plants and the current condition of your soil. Factors like budget and time availability influence the extent of amendments and techniques used. Despite the labor-intensive nature of soil amending, it is a vital step in creating a healthy and productive garden.

It's important to understand your existing soil type and its limitations before planting. As we move through the rest of this section, you'll learn that by working with your soil and not against it, you can make the type of growing environment that flourishes.

Tilth Soil and pH Levels

As a gardener, you may hear the words "*tilth soil*." Tilth soil is simply the physical condition of the soil as it relates to plant growth. The better your tilth, the better environment you have for your plants. There are a couple of ways to better understand tilth.

Physical tilth: This is the texture and structure of your soil. This will be your loam soil, as it's loose and crumbly, allowing for easy root penetration and water drainage.

Biological tilth: This is the activity and diversity of soil life, which includes microorganisms, earthworms, and insects. A healthy soil microbiome assists in nutrient cycling, decomposition, and the overall health of the soil.

You've seen an example of good tilth with loam soil, which has several benefits, such as enhanced seed germination and plant establishment, enhanced water infiltration and drainage, increased air circulation, and more available nutrients.

There are several things you can do to help create and maintain tilth.

Reduce tillage: Soil disturbance can lead to compaction, erosion, and loss of organic matter. Allow your soil to form aggregates naturally and improve its structure by either going to no-till or reduced-till gardening.

Add organic matter: Cover crops, manure, or compost can be used to improve soil structure, water retention, and available nutrients.

Practice crop rotation: Rotating different crops will help to stop disease cycles and improve the nutrient balance in your soil. You can also use a winter-covered crop to nourish the soil after your fall harvest.

Encourage a healthy microbiome: You can do this by adding compost tea, practicing biochar application, or using organic mulch. These things will allow the growth of beneficial microorganisms.

Now we come to soil pH levels and nutrient content, two crucial aspects of soil health that impact soil tilth and plant growth.

Soil pH: This is a measure of the acidity or alkalinity of your soil. Most plants are fit for soils that are slightly acidic to neutral on the pH scale (around 6.0 to 7.0).

Nutrient content: Your soil needs various macronutrients like nitrogen, phosphorus, and potassium. It also needs micronutrients like iron, zinc, and manganese to ensure healthy plant growth.

But how do you check your soil's health?

The most accurate method for assessing soil health is through soil testing, which can be done using a soil testing kit available at local garden centers. This kit will determine the pH level and nutrient content, guiding necessary amendments. Visual observation is also helpful; dark brown or black, crumbly soil with an earthy smell indicates good soil health. Poor plant growth and discoloration can indicate soil health issues as well. Once you understand your soil's condition, you can amend it accordingly. Adding mineral lime raises pH in acidic soil, while sulfur lowers it. Compost, manure, and fertilizers can address nutrient deficiencies while maintaining good tilth and encourages a healthy soil microbiome. Companion planting, especially nitrogen-fixing legumes, can also replenish soil nutrients. Additionally, companion planting enhances soil health by promoting a diverse plant community that improves nutrient utilization and attracts beneficial insects, which can help deter pests carrying harmful pathogens.

Preparing the Soil: Creating the Canvas

For every gardener, seasoned or beginner, proper soil preparation is the foundation for a successful and rewarding experience. This guide will help you get your soil ready for planting, and there will also be some time-saving tips and seasonal considerations.

First Steps

Keep in mind that certain aspects of your preparation may be omitted based on factors such as the current state of your soil, the size of your garden, and the climate. For instance, if you're utilizing raised garden beds or containers, you won't need to exert as much effort in soil preparation.

1. **Use the right timing.** You will want to prepare your soil at least four to six weeks before planting, during spring or fall. This timeframe will allow amendments like compost to break down and integrate with the rest of the soil.

2. **Test your soil.** For a successful garden, a soil test is essential for knowing pH levels and nutrient content. As we discussed earlier, the test results will allow you to make the correct amendments.

3. **Calculate your needs.** You can find a soil calculator at your local garden center or the following site https://soilcalcula tor.com/. It will help you estimate how many amendments you will need based on the size of your garden bed and the recommendations from your test. This saves time and money, as you will ensure you purchase the right amount of amendments.

4. **Clear and level the site.** You'll now have to move rocks, weeds, and other plant material. Use your rake to make a smooth planting surface.

5. **Loosen the soil.** Dig or till your soil to a depth of 8–12 inches. Remember to avoid over-tilling, as that could jeopardize your soil's tilth.

6. **Amend the soil.** Based on the results of your soil test, this will be the time to add amendments like compost, aged manure, or other organic matter. Try to add a two to three-inch layer that's spread evenly over the loosened soil. If you choose to use a pre-made fertilizer, make sure it meets your soil and plant needs (i.e., correct balance of macronutrients), as vegetables might need a different composition than flowers.

7. **Mix and refine:** Use your garden fork to thoroughly mix your amendments into the loosened soil and break up large chunks. When you're done, the soil should have a fine and crumbly texture.

8. **Let it settle.** Around two weeks before planting, you will want to water your prepared bed deeply. By doing this and allowing it to settle for one to two weeks before planting, you let the amendments break down even more, creating the optimal conditions for plant growth.

Improving Soil Structure

You want great soil tilth, so if you notice any discrepancies with your soil or plant growth, consider the following tips.

1. **Keep tilling to a minimum.** Remember, frequent tilling (turning over 8–10 inches of soil by hand or machine) damages soil aggregates, which leads to compaction, less air circulation, and less water infiltration. Reduce your tilling practices to once a year, or try to adopt no-till practices wherever you can.

2. **Use mulch.** Give the soil a two to three-inch layer of organic mulch like wood chips, shredded bark, or straw around your plants. This will help your soil retain moisture and suppress weeds. This type of mulch will also decompose, becoming organic matter that's added to the soil over time.

3. **Consider cover crops.** Crops like ryegrass, clover, or vetch can be beneficial during the off-season. They can help add nitrogen to the soil for fertility, prevent erosion, and suppress weeds. Then, right before they seed, you can till them under to add more organic material to the soil.

4. **Add compost:** While we will cover this more later, adding compost before planting will provide nutrients to the soil and improve its structure. You want to have at least a 2:1 ratio with two parts soil and one part compost. You'll spread this evenly over your garden bed before planting. Typically, you'll add more at least mid-way through the growth cycle.

Earthworms and insects can play an important role in improving your soil's structure and overall health, reducing the reliance on man-made fertilizers and pesticides.

Earthworms: As you dig in your soil, seeing earthworms is a good sign of soil health. These worms will aerate your soil as they make tunnels, which makes for better air and water movement. They also add to your nutrient cycle by breaking down organic matter and releasing nutrients to your plants. If you don't see any, add earthworms to your soil.

Beneficial insects: Ladybugs, lacewings, and ground beetles prey on harmful pests that could carry pathogens.

Seasonal Soil Preparations

Maintaining soil health is a year-round endeavor, which means there are steps you can take to ensure that your soil will always be ready for the growing season.

Winter

- **Protect the soil:** Cover garden beds with winter mulch (straw or leaves) to protect them from harsh weather. This cover will also help prevent soil erosion and maintain soil temperatures.

- **Plan ahead:** For those in the colder regions of your zone map, you can start seeds indoors, which will allow for early planting once spring arrives.

Spring

- **Soil testing:** Before you start planting for the new growing season, conduct a soil test in early spring to check nutrient levels. This will let you make amendments in a suitable time frame.

- **Prepare for planting:** You'll need to clean and level your garden. As the weather warms up, remove your winter mulch, make amendments, and water the beds.

- **Early planting:** Again, become familiar with your chosen plants and hardiness zone. Depending on your climate, you can start your garden with cool-season crops like lettuce, spinach, and peas.

Summer

- **Consistent mulching:** Maintain a layer of organic mulch around your plants during the summer. This will conserve moisture and suppress weed growth.

- **Top-dress:** In the event of heavy rain or a period of high watering, nutrients could leach out of the soil. Top-dressing is simply the practice of adding compost or a slow-release natural fertilizer over the top of the soil to replenish nutrients.

- **Harvest and replant:** As you harvest your vegetables over the summer, you can replant your fall crops (kale, radishes, or carrots).

Fall

- **Clean and amend:** After harvesting your fall crops, remove debris and plant matter from your garden beds. Use compost or composted manure to replenish nutrients and help soil structure.

- **Plant cover crops:** Using cover crops like clover, vetch, or ryegrass will protect your soil during the winter. They will add much-needed nitrogen, and it will become organic matter when you till them under your soil in the spring.

Additional Tips

Fun Tips

- **Marked tools:** Use paint or a Sharpie to mark ruler lines on your long tools. It will let you keep plants evenly spaced.

- **Healthy soil:** Add aged animal manure to the soil for improved health and fertility. This can be helpful if you don't have any compost.

Time-Saving Tips

- **Power drill planting:** Use an electric drill to become a power planter, speeding up the process.

- **Weed pulling:** Weed your garden when the soil is moist to allow easier removal.

We have now laid the groundwork for a successful and enjoyable gardening journey. This should serve as your reminder that taking time to gather tools and properly prepare your garden is crucial to seeing success. The groundwork you do before you plant and all year long will pay off for seasons to come.

Now that the garden is ready to go, we can start planting. In the next chapter, we will explore planting strategies.

***

Hey there, fellow plant enthusiasts!

Are you finding *The Complete Beginner's Guide to Companion Planting* enjoyable and informative? Is it inspiring your next steps to grow your bountiful garden? If so, why not share the excitement with others by leaving a review? Your feedback can help more gardening enthusiasts discover the value of this book!

Leaving a review for this book isn't just about sharing your thoughts; it's about helping others experience the same joy and fulfillment that you've found in your garden. Imagine the impact you could have on someone else's gardening journey and it could be the key to unlocking a world of possibilities for a fellow gardener.

Before you move on, take a few moments to leave your review. It's simple! Just scan the QR code or go online to where you purchased the book and click the "Write a Review" button. Share your thoughts, and you're done!

Your review could make all the difference for someone looking to enhance their garden. So, go ahead, leave a review, and let's spread the joy of companion planting together!

Chapter Five

Let's Get Planting

Everyday kitchen items can greatly benefit your garden. For instance, coffee grounds make excellent fertilizer, especially for acid-loving plants like tomatoes, blueberries, and azaleas. Rich in phosphorus, potassium, nitrogen, and magnesium, coffee grounds can also deter pests like slugs and snails. As noted by Abid (2023) in his blog, "10 Unusual Gardening Tips That Actually Work," these simple tips can help you create a thriving garden.

Now that you've prepared your garden design, companion plant list, garden tools, and soil, it's time to start planting. However, planting is not as simple as just putting plants in the ground, giving them water and sunlight, and hoping for the best. The next key to a successful garden lies in strategic planting, which involves more than just sowing seeds in rows.

In this chapter, we will explore various planting strategies that extend beyond traditional methods. We will discuss innovative techniques such as interplanting, where companion plants are strategically positioned to benefit each other, and succession planting, which maximizes harvests by utilizing space throughout the growing season. Keep in mind that not all techniques will work for every garden, as success depends on various factors. However, by understanding and implementing these strategies, you can improve the health and productivity of your garden.

Plant Spacing

Plant spacing is the strategic arrangement of plants in your garden, and it is an important component of a healthy, flourishing garden. Each plant requires a certain amount of space to grow and thrive due to the plant's size and growth rate. Arrange them so that each plant has adequate access to sunlight, water, nutrients, and air circulation.

Vegetable	Spacing (inches)	Vegetable	Spacing (inches)
Bush beans	4–6	Beets	2–3
Broccoli	12–18	Carrots	2–3
Corn	8–12	Bush cucumbers	12–18
Eggplant	18–24	Kale	12–18
Lettuce	8–12	Onions	2–3
Peas	2–3	Peppers	18–24
Potatoes (seed)	12–18	Pumpkins	60–100
Radishes	1–2	Spinach	4–6
Squash (winter)	36–60	Squash (summer)	12–18
Swiss Chard	12–18	Tomatoes (bush)	18–24
Turnips	3–4	Watermelons	60–100
Zucchini	36–60	Tomatoes (vining)	24–36

The Basics

Consider your plants as roommates in a shared living space. If you were to cram them all into a confined area, they would compete for resources such as nutrients, water, and sunlight. This competition often results in stunted growth and increases the risk of diseases. Therefore, it's crucial to understand the benefits of proper spacing for your plants. You will need to consider the following:

- **Adequate sunlight:** Sunlight is vital for photosynthesis. Overcrowding can completely shade out smaller plants, affecting their growth.

- **Air circulation:** While you want to retain moisture, too much buildup can lead to fungal diseases. Good circulation will prevent this from happening.

- **Access to water and nutrients:** Dense planting will quickly deplete the soil of vital resources, which will leave your plants weak and vulnerable.

Spacing Tips for Different Plant Types

With your garden and companion planting, you will have a variety of plants, and to keep them spaced properly, you should consider the following.

- **Vines:** Your climbing plants need vertical support, and you can find this with trellises or fences. Keep vining plants a few feet apart to allow proper vine expansion and to avoid overcrowding.

- **Perennials:** These are long-living plants, and they will get larger each year. You will need to consider their mature size when planting them to give them adequate space. For example, if you have a plant that will be three feet wide when mature, you will need to plant it at least three feet away from its neighbors.

- **Groundcovers:** These low-growing plants will be used to fill in bare spots and act as mulch. Spacing them closer (four to six inches) can allow for faster coverage, or you can adjust this to have a more controlled fill.

- **Annuals:** These plants will have much smaller mature sizes since they are short-lived. Space them by packaging instructions and keep in mind how they will grow (for example:

bushy or trailing).

Gardeners with limited space or those using raised beds or containers will still need to consider spacing despite these space restrictions.

- **Raised beds:** When you use raised beds, keep in mind that you're going to have limited soil depth. Therefore, look at your seed packets or plant tags, which will let you know if that plant will be suitable for your raised beds. If you're still unsure, then you can look for plants with shallow root systems or dwarf plants.

- **Container gardening:** Think about pot size when you're choosing plants. If you overcrowd containers, you will restrict root growth and impact drainage.

Vertical Spacing

Vertical spacing is the distance between plants at different heights. Your taller plants should be near the back of the bed or the "shadow side," then medium-sized plants, followed by low-growing varieties. The result will have a layered visual effect, but this spacing will ensure all plants get adequate sunlight. If in the Northern Hemisphere, taller plants towards the north side of the garden, and the opposite for those in the Southern Hemisphere.

Plant Spacing Chart

The following is a general guide for plant spacing for your most common plants. Specific spacing will vary depending on the variety of plants and growing conditions so check with local garden centers, growers, and packaging instructions.

Plant Bed Designs and Spacing Formulas

Three basic planting designs that work well for companion planting are shown in the illustration to help you get a better visualization for space. But remember, formulas for the designs still need to factor in the spacing needs of your plants listed on the seed packets. The designs include square, circle, and triangular spacing layouts, where the square design is the most common and easiest compared to the other layouts.

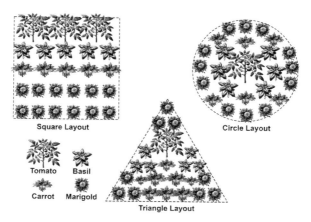

Plant bed designs: square, circle, and triangle.

- **Square beds:** A square bed is versatile and will work well with many planting practices, including companion planting. The only tip to follow is to make sure you're grouping plants that benefit each other.

  - Calculate the area of your garden bed (length x width) and divide that by the desired number of plants. The result will be the average spacing per plant.

- **Circular beds:** A circular design creates a focal point that is pleasing to the eye and suitable for companion planting. Arrange your plants in concentric circles based on height and light needs.

  - Divide the circumference of your circle by the number of plants. The result will let you determine the spacing between plant centers.

- **Triangular beds:** This design maximizes space usage and works amazingly with companion planting. This method simply places plants by staggering them. This can help keep weeds down; however, it's not chosen as often as it's not visually appealing for all designs.

  - Multiply the desired spacing of your plants with the square root of 3/2. Because this formula is a bit more complex, it's helpful to get the most accurate measurements by consulting dedicated apps or online calculators for triangular layouts.

Bonus Tip

For an even bigger boost in suppressing weeds, lay newspaper under your mulch. This technique will smother existing weeds and prevent new ones from sprouting. However, avoid using cardboard, as it contains chemicals that can be harmful to your garden.

Starting Seeds

Starting your garden from seeds lets you cultivate a wide array of plants, from flowers to fresh vegetables. This method gives you a unique yet rewarding experience. Planting from seeds gives you even more control over your plant selection and the quality of your plants, giving you a much deeper connection with the growing process.

There are several benefits to growing from seed, so let's look at a few of those.

- **Diversity and selection:** Again, seeds give you a much wider variety of plants compared to plants that are already established. It allows you to really get into the gardening world as you explore the unique and heritage varieties that aren't easy to find.

- **Cost-effective:** Growing from seeds is far cheaper than purchasing established plants, especially if your goal is a large quantity. For less than a mature plant, you can get a seed packet that has the potential to give you dozens of plants. While not every seed will germinate, it's still a more economical choice when you're gardening on a budget.

- **Fresher produce:** Growing from seeds will give you vegetables and herbs that taste better than many store-bought options. This is attributed to the ability to harvest them when they are at peak freshness and flavor.

- **Sense of accomplishment:** Witnessing the complete life cycle of a plant, from the seeds in the packet to a mature plant, gives any gardener immense satisfaction and a great feeling of accomplishment.

Planting From Seeds: A Step-by-Step Guide

Nothing will beat hands-on experience, but the following steps can carry you through your companion planting journey and beyond.

1. **Choose your seeds:** You want to choose high-quality seeds, and you should make sure they come from reputable sources. Your local garden centers are ideal because they will help you as you consider factors like your climate, desired harvest time, and preferred plant varieties. When you buy your seeds, make sure you check the packet for specific planting instructions. There will also be helpful germination information.

   ○ You can also join or host a seed swap with local growers. It is a great way to connect with other gardeners in the area, acquire new seeds, and exchange valuable information.

2. **Prepare your seed starting mix:** You'll also pick this up at

your garden center. Opt for a sterile, well-draining starting mix made for seedlings. It will allow the right amount of moisture retention and aeration for the delicate early stages.

3. **Select containers:** Choose containers with drainage holes to avoid waterlogging, which is harmful to seedlings. You can even use recycled containers like yogurt cups, cardboard tubes, or egg cartons; they are suitable options for starting seeds indoors.

4. **Planting the seeds:** Moisten the seed-starting mix well and fill the containers. From there, you will sow the seeds according to the recommended depth and spacing (that's on the packet). Lightly cover the seeds with the mix and firm up the surface. Be careful not to compact the mix during that last step.

5. **Watering and light:** Gently water your seeds with a spray bottle and avoid disturbing them. You'll need to keep your eye on this because the seeds need consistent moisture, but overwatering could cause rot. Give your seeds adequate sunlight, or use artificial grow lights.

6. **Germination and thinning:** Once your seedlings emerge, you will need to adjust watering to match their needs. As they grow, it's helpful to thin out the new sprouts by removing some of them. This prevents overcrowding and ensures that the remaining seedlings have enough space for healthy development.

7. **Transplanting:** There will be a larger section on this, but once your seedlings establish several sets of true leaves, you

can transplant them into larger pots or your garden beds.

Seasonal Planting Chart

As you saw in step one, planting seeds strategically based on your climate and desired harvest time is crucial if you want success. Use your hardiness zone maps and other seasonal planting charts (like we included earlier) to determine the ideal sowing times. Keep in mind, especially for those in colder regions, that you should consider when the last frost of the winter will come. It will help you find a good seed-starting schedule. You can also use one of the following sites that will help you even further.

- Territorial Seed Company: https://territorialseed.com/blogs/spring-growing-guides

- The Seed Collection: https://www.theseedcollection.com.au/assets/files/TheSeedCollection-%20Sowing%20Chart.pdf

Additional Seeding Tips

- **Pre-moisten your seeds.** Soak your seeds in water overnight or for a few hours before planting. The length of the time is determined by seed variety, but It helps speed up the germination process.

- **Label your containers.** Label your containers clearly with the plant name, sowing date, water needs (after germination), and any other relevant information. It will help you stay organized and avoid giving improper care to your plants.

- **Invest in a heat mat.** Using a heat mat can promote faster germination for seeds that need warmer soil temperatures. You may also get a boost in germination from a growth lamp.

- **Sprinkle cinnamon on your starting mix:** Cinnamon's potential antifungal properties can combat seedling rot. After placing your seeds in the starting mix, lightly sprinkle cinnamon on top to prevent direct contact with the seeds.

Common Seeding Mistakes and How to Avoid Them

- **Overwatering:** Make sure you give your seeds proper drainage. Only water the top layer of the soil when it's dry to the touch. Use a spray bottle to mist the soil without disturbing the seeds.

- **Insufficient light:** Your seedlings need adequate light, even when you're starting them indoors. Insufficient light exposure can lead to slowed growth and weaker plants.

- **Not thinning seedlings:** As they germinate and sprout through the soil thin your seedlings as directed to avoid overcrowding. You must ensure proper air circulation and nutrients are being provided to your plants.

- **Ignoring temperature requirements:** While you can start your seeds indoors, you still need to be mindful of the temperature range on the seed packet. Making things too hot or cold can hinder or kill your seedlings.

Transplanting

Transplanting is a fundamental gardening practice where a plant is moved from one location to another. Every gardener should be familiar with this technique. The most common example of transplanting is starting seeds indoors and later transplanting the young plants to their final growing locations, whether it's a garden bed or a larger pot. If you decide to buy young plants from a garden store or grower, you'll need to transplant them from the trays to your garden. Mastering this process is essential for ensuring that your plants thrive in their new environment.

Why Transplant?

While some regions and certain plants can be sown directly outdoors, transplanting gives you several advantages.

- **Controlled environment:** Your plants will benefit a lot from beginning their growth in a controlled indoor environment because they are protected from harsh weather and pests until they are hardy enough to handle them.

- **Early start:** With transplants, you extend your growing season, perfect for those with short summers. It also works well for those who want to harvest earlier and those who just want to enjoy longer blooming periods.

- **Stronger plants:** Your plants will develop a much stronger root system because of the controlled environment. It gives you healthier and more productive plants throughout the season.

When Do You Transplant?

Knowing when to move your plants to their new home will depend on a few factors.

- **Plant type:** Each plant variety will have specific requirements. Again, you'll find these on your seed packet, or you will have gained that information through other growers or your local garden center.

- **Climate:** Average temperatures and your region's frost dates will play a role in the timing of your transplanting.

- **Seedling size and maturity:** You should wait until your seedlings have developed several sets of their true leaves. The plants should also be at least a couple of inches tall before transplanting.

The Transplanting Process

1. **Ready your planting area.** Make sure the soil of your garden bed (or other location) is loose, fertile, and clean of weeds. Remember that this is the time to amend the soil with compost or other organic matter, depending on your soil tests.

2. **Harden your seedlings.** As the organic matter breaks down, filling your soil with nutrients, start acclimating your seedlings to outdoor conditions. Take time to expose them to increasing periods of sunlight, wind, and outdoor tem-

peratures. This process should take a week or two.

3. **Water thoroughly.** Young transplants will need a thorough watering one to two days before transplanting them. This makes it easier to remove them from the starting containers.

4. **Dig the hole.** In your garden bed or container, dig a hole in the prepared soil slightly bigger than your seedlings' root ball.

5. **Carefully remove the seedling from the starting container.** Squeeze the sides of the container gently. It will loosen the root ball for planting. If the seedling is pot-bound, loosen the roots near the edges with a fork. Protecting your roots will encourage outward growth in the new soil.

6. **Plant the seedling in its new home.** Place the seedling in the hole you dug. It should be around the same level as it was in the container. Gently backfill the area with soil and gently firm it around the base of the plant.

7. **Water the transplants.** Water the new transplants generously. It will help settle the soil and ensure the roots make good contact with the soil.

Tips for Successful Transplanting

- **Gently handle seedlings:** Seedlings are very delicate, even when you've hardened them to your garden's condition. Minimize stress on the plants by working quickly (and carefully) during the process.

- **Transplant at the right time:** Transplant your seedlings on a cloudy day or in the evening. It can help reduce any shock caused by a transplant.

- **Be water-wise:** Keep your seedlings consistently watered during the first few weeks. Giving them enough moisture will help them become established.

- **Monitor your seedlings:** Watch your plants closely for signs of stress. If you notice any wilting or drooping leaves, give the seedlings shade or additional water to help them.

- **Use mulch to protect your plants:** Place a layer of mulch around the base of your transplants. It will protect them by suppressing weeds and regulating soil temperatures. It will also help by retaining moisture.

- **Lightly fertilize:** Consider using a diluted liquid fertilizer to give your seedlings a boost. You will do this a few weeks after transplanting when young plants begin to show new growth.

- **Protect from pests:** Be proactive in pest control because they can also target your seedlings. While companion planting helps, you can go beyond that by setting up row covers in the early stages as the plants mature. It will save your seedlings and young plants.

Succession Planting

While companion planting focuses on the strategic positioning of your plants to benefit each other, succession planting complements this by maximizing the use of space through multiple plantings throughout the season. This dynamic duo allows you to create a thriving and productive garden that gives yield throughout the year.

What Is Succession Planting?

Succession planting is a gardening technique that involves planting different crops in the same space at different times throughout the growing season. This method ensures a continuous harvest and maximizes garden productivity. There are various ways to implement succession planting, such as replacing harvested crops with new ones, staggering plantings for a continuous harvest, growing different crops together, or planting the same crop with varying maturity dates for a prolonged harvest. We'll discuss the different ways in more depth, but each approach offers unique benefits to optimize garden space and resources.

Benefits of Succession Planting

- **Higher productivity:** When you use the same space multiple times in one growing season, you will significantly increase your overall yield. This is much higher compared to just planting a single crop and letting the space go unused for the rest of the year after harvesting.

- **Extended harvest window:** You can harvest longer by planting fast-maturing crops followed by slower-maturing varieties. It will let you enjoy a continuous supply of garden-fresh vegetables.

- **Efficiently use space:** Succession planting makes the most of your available space, especially in smaller gardens. With the right planning, you will maximize your garden's potential, even with limited resources.

- **Improved soil health:** You can plant different crops in one growing area, and it will still count as crop rotation. Nutrients will still be replenished, which will keep the soil healthy for several planting seasons.

Planning for Succession Planting

- **Know your growing season:** Knowing the first and last frost dates in your region will help you determine optimal planting times for your different crops.

- **Choose your crops:** Select a mix of fast-maturing and slow-maturing vegetables whose planting needs complement each other. You might want to incorporate beans and peas into the rotation because these nitrogen-fixing plants can improve soil fertility.

- **Plan your planting schedule:** Create a chart outlining the crops, when to plant them, and the expected dates for them to mature. The following chart is just an example as every region and garden will be different.

Crop	Planting Dates	Maturity Days	Harvest Dates
Radishes	Early Spring	28	Mid-Spring
Lettuce	Early Spring	45	Mid-to-Late Spring
Spinach	Early Spring	40	Mid-to-Late Spring
Bush beans	Late Spring	55	Early Summer
Summer Squash	Late Spring	50	Mid-Summer
Cherry Tomatoes	Late Spring	60	Mid-Summer to Early Fall
Kale	Late Summer	55	Fall
Arugula	Late Summer	30	Fall

Succession Planting Methods

- **Same crop, staggered plantings:** You can opt to plant the same crop, except you will plant those seeds every few weeks to ensure a continuous harvest.

- **Different plants, same space:** Plant your fast-maturing crops like spinach, basil, or radishes between your slower-maturing plants like tomatoes or peppers. It will allow you to harvest the fast-maturing crops before the slower ones need the space.

- **Three Sisters method:** This method brings the principles of companion planting and unifies it with succession planting completely.

- **Same plant, multiple varieties:** This involves planting varieties of the same crop with different maturity dates, which will extend your harvesting window. For example, plant varieties (early, mid, and late season) of tomatoes or lettuce to enjoy the same vegetables for a longer period. Be aware of your zone. Colder regions may not have adequate growing time for multiple plants and harvesting.

Additional Tips for Succession Planting

- **Start seeds inside:** This is what we discussed at the beginning of the chapter. By starting indoors, you get an early harvest and a jumpstart on the growing season.

- **Directly sow some crops:** For those plants that will mature quickly, consider planting them directly outdoors. Keep in mind to do this at the appropriate times (by seed packet instructions) throughout the season.

- **Make regular amendments to your soil:** Regularly add compost or organic matter to your soil to maintain its fertility and support year-round for beautiful gardens, building the tilth up over the years and improving soil structure.

- **Follow your spacing guidelines:** Follow the recommended spacing guidelines for your crops to ensure they have air circulation and can grow properly.

- **Clear harvested crops promptly:** After one crop has finished producing, remove it from your garden to open up space for new plantings. This will also be a proactive measure to stop the spread of diseases.

Planting Strategies for Abundance

Once you have your garden site prepared, you're ready to practice companion planting. We've discussed how certain plants will mutually benefit one another, like taller plants offering shade to heat-sensitive plants or repelling harmful insects from neighboring plants. But now, let's think of some other strategies that could ramp up your companion garden's results.

- **Polyculture:** Polyculture is an advanced form of companion planting that mimics natural ecosystems by planting different species together. This approach fosters biodiversity, attracting beneficial insects while deterring pests. For example, planting tomatoes, basil, and marigolds together in the same bed can create a polyculture. Tomatoes provide a tall canopy, basil acts as a pest repellent and improves tomato flavor, while marigolds deter nematodes. This symbiotic relationship among plants enhances overall garden health and productivity.

- **The rule of opposites (complementarity):** Planting plants with different nutrient needs and root depths in the same area could give you optimal resource utilization. The best example here is using deep-rooted legumes to fix nitrogen in the soil, which benefits shallow-rooted vegetables.

- **KISS (Keep It Simple, Silly):** Remember to start with something small and manageable, especially with your first companion garden. Keep your focus on a few plant varieties that you're interested in. You can gradually expand your garden from here as you gain experience and confidence.

While these things together will maximize effectiveness, you should spend a good amount of time on site preparation. You could implement any strategy you wanted, but they would struggle if the site doesn't have what those plants need to flourish, brings us to one of the most important parts of site preparation: preparing the soil.

Interactive Element: Making a Planting Calendar and Growth Chart

Planning your garden is essential to your success. With a planting calendar, you can ensure that your seeds and seedlings are started and planted at the right time. It will take a little work, but here's how you can create your own calendar and growth chart.

Planting Calendar

- **Step 1: Gather information:** You will need to explore your resources, either online, in person, or through your local gardening center. These are things that we have discussed already, but let's refresh on the following:

  - **Your hardiness zone:** No matter where you are in the world, you should know your hardiness zone because your region's minimum winter temperature is crucial for determining plant viability and planting times.

  - **Frost dates:** It's important to know the dates of your first and last frosts. These dates indicate when temperatures are likely to drop below freezing. Many vegetable varieties are vulnerable to frost and freezing conditions.

Planting too early or too late in the season can impact plant growth and the overall harvest. Understanding the frost dates will help you plan your growing season and make informed decisions about planting frost-sensitive plants.

- ○ **Planting times:** Knowing the recommended planting times for your plant varieties will also help fill out your calendar. Keep in mind these times will depend on the growth cycle of the plant, sensitivity to frost, and maturity rates.

- **Step 2: Organize your calendar:** Choose a format that works best for you. You can use the calendar app on your phone, or you can use a physical calendar that hangs near your gardening tools. Your first markings are going to be your first and last frost dates.

- **Step 3: Plan your plantings:** Based on your research and your desired harvest times, begin mapping out when you want to start your seeds indoors, transplant dates, and dates for direct planting. Seed packets usually contain information about the number of days to plant maturity, plant spacing (useful for companion planting), and light requirements.

- **Step 4: Personalize and adapt:** This is your calendar, which means it should be fit for you! Add notes and reminders about specific tasks, and amend them as much as you need.

Plant Growth Chart

- **Step 1: Set up your chart:** Sketch or use your computer to create a table with the following columns.

  - Plant Name

  - Plant Date

  - Germination Date (if applicable)

  - Transplant Date (if applicable)

  - Growth Stages (seedling, vegetative, flowering, fruiting, etc.)

  - Observations and Notes

The following is a rough idea of your growth chart. Remember to leave enough room to write in information.

Plant Name	Plant Date	Germination Date (if applicable)	Transplant Date (if applicable)	Growth stages	Observations and notes

- **Step 2: Track your progress:** As your plants grow, fill out your chart. Track their progress in the "observations and notes" section. Some information you can track here would be:

  - seedling emergence

- ○ leaf development, including the first set of true leaves

- ○ flowering or fruiting

- ○ signs of stress, pests, or diseases

- **Step 3: Utilize your observations:** Your notes and observations will be used to make decisions in the future. Besides knowing what works and what doesn't for next year's garden, you can:

  - ○ Look at growth patterns and adjust planting times to benefit your garden and the plants.

  - ○ Gain a deeper knowledge about the specific needs of each plant and the varieties of those plants.

  - ○ Recognize and handle any problems when they start.

We have explored the fundamentals of planting for your companion garden from starting seeds to germination and transplanting, and you've even learned about the benefits of using succession planning. Remember to start small, keep it simple, and build upon your skills over the years. So now, let's turn our attention to taking care of your plants. In the next chapter, we will explore the world of water management, exploring irrigation techniques for your garden.

Chapter Six

Water Strategies for Successful Gardens

The article, *How Plants Use Water*, highlights the fact that water is an essential nutrient for plants, comprising up to 95% of a plant's tissue. It is required for seed germination, nutrient transport, photosynthesis, and maintaining turgor pressure in plant cells (Richmond, 2021).

Picture your vegetable garden as a sensory feast, captivating all five senses. As you move through the rows, your fingers brush against the soft leaves of lettuce and the prickly vines of a cucumber plant. The air is alive with the earthy aroma of freshly turned soil and the sweet scent of ripening tomatoes. You can hear the gentle rustle of the wind through the corn stalks and the chirping of birds. The vibrant colors of ripe peppers, glossy eggplants, and plump strawberries catch your eye, tempting you to taste their fresh, flavorful bounty. Every sense is delighted, making the experience of growing and harvesting your food truly rewarding. Your planning and planting techniques have paid off, as has your understanding of one of the most critical elements for sustaining the ecosystem: water.

Water is the essential lifeblood of every garden. Like humans, plants rely on this resource to survive and thrive. Managing water for a successful garden goes beyond keeping the soil moist. In this chapter, you'll learn the critical role water plays in gardening. We will explore efficient practices and some innovative solutions, like how companion planting will reduce water usage while saving time and costs for cultivating a healthy, sustainable garden.

So what better way to get started with a chapter all about watering your garden than by understanding your water needs?

Understanding Water Needs

You already know that your plants need water, but when you understand why your plants need it and how they use it, it can make you more aware of individual watering needs over just getting the soil wet and forgetting it.

The Importance of Water in Gardening

- **Essential for plant growth:** Plants are made up of cells and tissues, and one of the building blocks of those elements is water. Water forms the base of sap, which transports nutrients and minerals through the plant, giving it what it needs to grow and develop. Without adequate water, the growth of cells will slow down or stall completely, hindering the plant's overall growth. It will lead to stunted or underdeveloped plants.

- **Temperature regulation:** Water is a natural coolant for plants, helping them regulate internal temperature, which is crucial during the hot summer months. As we will learn more later, plants prevent overheating through a process known as transpiration. It's a process that is much like sweating in humans. When your plants maintain optimal temperatures, their vital functions go uninterrupted.

- **Maintains plant structure:** Water gives plants structural support to their cells. This is what gives plants rigidity and helps them keep their upright position. Without a sufficient amount of water, plants will wilt and go limp. Think of a stalk of celery, for example. It's crispy because of the high water content in its cells. Without water, that stalk would just fall over in your hands.

- **Facilitates photosynthesis:** Water plays a huge role in this important process. Along with sunlight and carbon dioxide, these elements are converted to energy in the form of glucose. Water is vital to this process because the molecules are split, providing the hydrogen needed to make glucose, which fuels plant growth and development.

- **Promotes nutrient uptake:** Water dissolves the nutrients in the soil, making them available to absorb through their roots. Without water, the nutrients stay in the soil, inaccessible to your plants, which will impact their ability to grow.

How Plants Use Water

Plants absorb water through their roots, which then travels through the xylem (a network of tubes) to reach all parts of the plant. Water plays a vital role in two important plant functions: transpiration and photosynthesis.

- **Transpiration:** This process involves the release of water vapor through the stomata, which are tiny pores on the leaves. While it may sound like water loss, it is crucial for the health of your plant. As discussed earlier, transpiration regulates plant temperature, prevents waterlogging, and contributes to overall plant health. When water evaporates from the leaves, it creates a pulling effect that draws more water up from the roots, maintaining a constant flow of water throughout the plant.

- **Photosynthesis:** Photosynthesis is a fundamental process for growing vegetables as it is how plants convert sunlight into energy, fueling their growth and development. Sunlight provides the energy needed to convert carbon dioxide from the air and water from the soil into glucose, a form of sugar that plants use as food. This process not only allows plants to produce their food but also releases oxygen into the atmosphere as a byproduct, benefiting the environment.

Of course, there is also nutrient uptake, as water breaks the nutrients in the soil down to make them available to plants. You know from our chapter on soil that the present nutrients are vital to the development of your garden.

Understanding the vital role water plays in your garden's development will help you find better success. Let's use this knowledge to further understand water requirements, watering techniques, watering challenges, and schedules to foster healthy and thriving plants.

Plant Water Requirements

Your garden's needs are very similar to human needs when it comes to water. For instance, consider the difference between someone who is sedentary and a bodybuilder. The bodybuilder requires more nutrients and water daily, whereas the sedentary individual needs water but not as much. Your plants have similar needs! Every gardener understands that thriving plants require the right amount of water. However, with the wide variety of plants that can be grown, determining the correct amount of water can be challenging. This is where understanding hydrophytes, mesophytes, and xerophytes becomes important. These terms describe the water requirements of plants and can further assist you in establishing your garden.

Hydrophytes: The Water Lovers

- **What they are:** These are plants that have adapted to aquatic environments, meaning there is always water available to them. It also makes them very delicate by nature.

- **Habitat:** These plants thrive in or near ponds, lakes, rivers, and other freshwater sources, meaning they aren't ideal for areas that aren't their native homes.

- **Garden adaptations:** None, as they are not meant for traditional gardens where plants grow in soil.

- **Plant structure:** Many of these plants lack a strong root system, so they rely on abundant water for support and nutrient uptake.

- Cuticle (waxy layer on the leaves): Absent or thin because hydrophytes don't need it because of their constant access to water.

- **Leaves:** Can be thin and submerged, which lets gases exchange underwater. The leaves can also be broad and floating to maximize sunlight absorption.

- **Examples:** Water lilies, lotus, water hyacinths, hornwort, bladderworts

Mesophytes

: A Majority of Plants

- **What they are:** Mesophytes are plants that have adapted to moderate water availability, and they make up a majority of our garden plants. They thrive in areas with average rainfall or consistent irrigation.

- **Ideal zone for growth:** Most garden plants will be in this category; they encompass a wide range of zones.

- **Garden adaptations:** Implement a regular watering schedule, especially during hot or dry spells, soil amendment depending on the quality and plant needs, mulch and other techniques to slow evaporation and keep soil moist.

- **Plant structure:** Mesophytes have well-developed root and shoot systems, which help the plant capture water and nutrients from your fertile soil.

  ○ **Cuticle:** The waxy layer is a moderate thickness, which provides a balance between regulating water loss and allowing gasses to be exchanged.

  ○ **Leaves:** These plants will have diverse leaves with various sizes, shapes, and textures. It all depends on the specific plant and the function of the leaves (photosynthesis, transpiration, etc.).

- **Examples:** Tomatoes, beans, sunflowers, roses, many vegetables and herbs, ornamental grasses, ferns, and many varieties of trees.

Xerophytes: Plants for a Dryer Climate

- **What they are:** These plants have adapted to dry environments and little water availability. Xerophytes thrive in arid climates, sandy soils, and areas that get little water (irrigation or rainfall).

- **Ideal zone for growth:** If you live in a drier climate with low rainfall or sandy soil, you have a suitable habitat for these plants as long as you implement mindful watering practices.

- **Garden adaptations:** May need infrequent watering in dry times. These plants thrive on an average of one to two inches of rainwater a year in most cases.

- **Plant structure:** Xerophytes have an extensive root system, allowing them to access water stored deep in the soil.

    ○ **Reduced foliage:** These plants have less foliage to minimize the surface area. By doing this, the plant can reduce water loss through transpiration.

    ○ **Cuticle:** The cuticle on xerophytes is thick and waxy, and it acts as a barrier, keeping water loss from the few leaves it does have to a minimum.

    ○ **Leaves:** The leaves found on these plants have adapted and are small, spiny, or scale-like. This is also to minimize water loss.

- **Examples:** Cacti, succulents (aloe vera, jade plant), rosemary, lavender, yuccas, agaves, olive trees, sagebrush

Three plant types with different watering needs.

Watering Techniques

Effectively watering your garden is more than just turning on the watering hose. Using the right watering technique can save water and time, and it will ensure your plants' success. Let's break down the popular methods and how to choose the one that's right for your garden.

Watering Methods

- **Misting:** Great for plants that love humidity, like ferns and greenhouses. However, this is not your most efficient method because it loses water to evaporation. It also doesn't give you the deep watering your roots need.

- **Watering can:** This method is great for targeted watering, especially for newly planted seedlings or container plants. A good method, but it can be time-consuming if you have a large garden and run the risk of overwatering.

- **Bottom watering:** This method is when you take your pots and place them in a shallow dish filled with water. Your plant will absorb the water through the drainage holes. It's great for avoiding waterlogging and even promoting root growth. Use this method more for your houseplants.

- **Garden hose:** This method is versatile and cost-effective, but it does run a higher risk of being wasteful and causing mold, rot, or other diseases if they are not monitored. If using a garden hose, use a watering wand or nozzle for better control and to avoid overwatering.

- **Sprinklers:** These are great for large areas, but they can be inefficient because of evaporation and uneven watering. You should also avoid using this method on windy days or in areas with shallow-rooted plants.

- **Soaker hoses:** You can lie perforated hoses along your plant rows. It allows slow and even water distribution directly to the roots of your plants. Soaker hoses are great for areas that need to conserve water.

- **Drip irrigation:** This is the most efficient method. A network of tubes and emitters will directly deliver water to the roots, which means very little evaporation and waste. It's the ideal method for large gardens, vegetable patches, and irregularly shaped beds.

How to Choose the Right Method for You

With so many methods, it can be a bit difficult to know which method will be the most effective for your garden.

- **Consider plant type:** Deep-rooted plants like kale will benefit from gradual flow or soaker hoses. Your shallow-rooted plants, though, will prefer frequent, light watering.

- **Factor in climate:** If you are in a hot, dry climate, drip irrigation or soaker hoses are ideal because they will minimize evaporation. Cool, humid areas, though, can thrive from watering cans or gradual flow.

- **Soil type:** Think back to what we learned about soil. Sandy soil will drain quickly, requiring more frequent watering, while clay retains water, needing less watering.

Tips for Watering Efficiency

- **Water deeply and less frequently.** Try to soak the root zone and not just the surface. The root zone is where the nutrients will be broken down and fed into the plant.

- **Water in the early morning or later evenings.** This will help keep water loss due to evaporation at a minimum.

- **Use mulch around plants.** This will suppress weeds that would compete for water, and it will retain moisture.

- **Group plants with similar needs.** Again, companion planting will be a tremendous way to simplify watering and avoid competition. Plants with larger leaves will provide shade for more water-conserving companion plants underneath.

- **Learn your plants' specific needs.** Just as we have discussed already, different plants have varying requirements. By knowing what those are before you plant, you will already have the method chosen that works best.

Bonus Tips

- **A spot of tea:** While not a watering method, a fun trick for your new seedlings is to mist them with a cool chamomile tea every day. This gives them the gentle watering they need, but the anti-fungal properties of the tea can help prevent what is known as damping off (a common seedling disease).

- **Repurposed water:** This is also known as greywater use, and it's when you redirect water from your laundry and handwashing sinks through a filter and water your garden. If you have a fish tank, you can also use the water you take out for your plants.

Watering Challenges

Even when you try your best, watering challenges can still happen. Recognizing the signs and taking immediate corrective action will prevent any lasting damage to your plants.

Signs of Overwatering

- **Wilting or drooping leaves:** This issue can also come from underwatering, but overwatering will cause wilting because of root damage.

- **Yellowing leaves:** This one is easy to spot, but besides turning yellow, leaves may fall prematurely.

- **Soft, mushy stems:** Overly moist soil will cause stem rot, which can lead to this issue.

- **Mold or fungus growth:** Excess moisture or lack of airflow can turn your plants into a breeding ground for mold and fungus. You'll find most of this growth on the plants' leaves and growing on top of your soil.

- **Stunted growth:** A common mistake is overwatering because you believe you're helping your plants grow. However, the roots of the plant may be damaged, which causes them to struggle to absorb nutrients.

Reviving Overwatered Plants

1. *Stop watering immediately!* Let your soil completely dry.

2. Look for ways to improve your drainage. You can check for clogged drainage holes in your pots. If you've planted in the ground, consider a raised bed or container filled with amended soil.

3. If you leave the plant in the ground, use this time to aerate the soil around the base of the plant with a small fork. It will improve air circulation.

4. If necessary, you will need to remove any brown or mushy parts of your plant. It will help prevent potential disease outbreaks.

5. In the event of compacted or soggy soil, try repotting in fresh, well-draining soil. When moving your plant, check and remove any mushy roots.

Signs of Underwatering

- **Dry, crispy leaves:** You'll see leaves become dry, brittle, and curling inward.

- **Drooping and wilting:** You will see your leaves and stems go limp as they lose their water content.

- **Stunted growth:** Under-watered plants show slowed growth and smaller leaves.

- **Visibly dry soil:** The soil surface will be noticeably dry, and if it's in a pot, it will easily pull away from the edges.

Reviving Underwatered Plants

1. Water the plant deeply and slowly. Do not pour water onto the soil. Give the water time to soak in, and just use a gentle flow until you see soil run out of the drainage holes (in a pot) or until the top inch of soil is moist.

2. You can also mist the leaves, which can be helpful in hot or dry climates. This will give the under-watered plant temporary moisture until the roots absorb the water.

3. Group plants together, which can help retain moisture. Keep in mind that they need to have similar water needs.

4. Mulch around the plants if you haven't already. A good mulch will help retain soil moisture and reduce evaporation.

Seasonal and Weather Adjustments

- **Spring:** In the spring you'll start out watering lightly and gradually increase the amount as your plants grow and temperatures rise.

- **Summer:** Increase the frequency of watering plants due to higher temperatures and increased evaporation. Avoid watering in the heat of the day, the best times are either in the morning or evening.

- **Fall:** As temperatures and sun angles start to wane, you'll taper your watering off as you harvest your garden and plants start going dormant.

- **Winter:** Depending on your climate zone, watering can be stopped or greatly reduced since most plants go dormant and need less water. This is a good time to give your garden a rest, until the next growing season.

- **Windy days:** Increase watering frequency because the wind dries out the soil faster and the loose, dry soil can burn your plants' leaves.

- **Rainy days:** You can skip watering if the soil feels sufficiently moist.

Avoid Watering Mistakes

- **Watering schedule:** A schedule can be helpful, but if you only follow the schedule and ignore factors like weather and the plant type, you might be making a huge mistake. Always check the soil moisture before watering.

- **Not considering container plants:** Clay pots can dry out faster, which means they need frequent watering.

- **Improper drainage:** Make sure your pots and soil are well-draining to avoid root rot.

- **Overwatering young plants:** Young plants need to be kept moist, not soggy.

Water Saving Strategies

Watering your garden not only drives up your water bill but can have a significant impact on the global water supply. While it might seem that the water we use in our gardens, whether in a city or rural setting, is inconsequential on a large scale, the cumulative effect is significant. For instance, in urban areas, excessive watering can strain city water supplies, leading to increased water costs and potential shortages. Additionally, runoff from gardens in urban and rural areas can contribute to water pollution, affecting the quality of rivers, lakes, and groundwater. This pollution can harm aquatic life and affect the overall health of the ecosystem. Therefore, gardeners need to be mindful of their water usage and its environmental impact, recognizing that their actions can have far-reaching consequences on the environment. Grouping your plants with similar water needs together is one of the benefits of companion planting, but there are a few other things you can do to save as much water as you can.

- **Choose drought-tolerant plants:** Look for plants that naturally require less water.

- **Use a moisture meter:** This relatively inexpensive tool can help you determine the moisture level in your soil. It saves water and reduces the chances of overwatering.

- **Fix leaky faucets and hoses:** There's a high chance that your water waste comes from unnecessary leaks. Monitor your faucets and hoses and promptly fix issues when they arise.

Rainwater Collection

Another way you can save water is through rainwater collection, a simple water conservation method. It's not only great at lowering your water bill, but it comes in handy during the arid summer months or periods of water restriction. However, the biggest advantage is that you're giving natural water to your plants. Rainwater is usually soft and free of chlorine, which is generally better for your plants.

This approach uses rain barrels or cisterns that will collect the water from your roof's gutters. Install a filter on top of the barrel to keep out debris, and take proactive measures to prevent mosquito breeding.

Creating a Watering Schedule Chart

A watering schedule serves as a guide and a reminder to engage with your garden. It's a helpful tool for assessing the overall health of your garden and its water needs. By visually inspecting the plants' foliage and soil moisture, and considering the weather patterns, you can determine how much water to supplement. Importantly, a watering schedule does not always indicate that the garden needs water; rather, it prompts you to assess its water requirements. It's crucial to remember that while a watering chart can be beneficial, relying solely on it can lead to overwatering or underwatering your plants. Therefore, use it as a guide and a reminder, and always check your soil moisture before watering each plant.

How to Make Your Chart

1. **Identify your plants:** List all the plants you have in your garden.

2. **Identify their water needs:** Remember to use online databases, local garden centers, or seed packets to determine each plant's watering needs (daily, weekly, etc.).

3. **Fill out your chart:** For every plant you have, your chart should have the name of the plant, recommended watering frequency, and special notes like "prefers morning waterings" or "likes moist soil."

4. **Adjust based on weather:** To avoid overwatering and underwatering, adjust your watering to the weather. You will water more frequently when it's hot and dry, and you will reduce watering during cool or rainy weather.

5. **Monitor your plants:** Always check your plants for signs of thirst or overwatering. Adjust your schedule as needed.

Sample Chart

Plant Name	Watering Frequency	Notes
Tomato	Daily	Water the roots and avoid getting the leaves wet.
Pepper	Every other day	If leaves start to droop, reduce watering.
Lettuce	Weekly	Needs deep watering to reach the roots.

While your soil gives your plants a great foundation, you can't grow a garden without water, and throughout this chapter, you have been equipped with the knowledge and tools to navigate your plants' hydration needs. Adopting proper watering techniques is the foundation for healthy plant growth. When you can give your plants the right amount of water at the right time, you encourage strong root development, vibrant foliage, and ideal flowering or fruiting.

Remember, this chapter provides a general blueprint, but there are countless regions and unique gardens, allowing for plenty of room for exploration and experimentation. Don't hesitate to fine-tune your watering strategy based on the specific needs of your plants and your region. While you may need to make significant adjustments, closely observing your plants and watching for subtle cues will guide you. There is no one-size-fits-all approach to watering, similar to every other aspect of gardening. The key is to be adaptable and have a good understanding of what you're growing. Now that your setup and growing techniques are established, we can move on to maintaining your garden, which will ultimately lead to an abundant harvest.

Chapter Seven

Easy Garden Maintenance for Abundant Harvests

Remember our gardener from the introduction? She was overwhelmed by an empty garden and a vast field of advice. All she wanted was a vibrant, productive garden that could easily be maintained. That's when she discovered the concept of companion planting. It piqued her curiosity, so she planted basil and carrots between her tomatoes and nasturtiums near her peppers to deter pests.

The results were surprising to her. Her basil grew rather quickly. The carrots broke up the soil for her tomatoes making them grew taller. She didn't see a single aphid on her plants. The nasturtiums thrived, giving her garden pockets of color, and welcomed some beneficial insects. It inspired her to experiment more by interplanting cucumbers with her corn, giving the vines a place to climb.

The journey wasn't always smooth sailing. She had some challenges with watering adjustments, which caused some moments of doubt. But with each season, she learned more, adjusted her approach, and witnessed how companion planting greatly improved her garden. Now, her garden is a collection of healthy and robust plants, a testament to what learning, effort, and consistency will lead to.

Having learned how to establish your soil, select the right plants, and navigate watering challenges, you're now ready to tackle the maintenance required and maximize your harvest.

Composting

Composting is a time-honored technique for converting food scraps and yard waste into a nutrient-rich additive for your garden. This "black gold" not only helps you save money but also nourishes your plants and benefits the environment. To create healthy compost, you need to maintain the right ratio of carbon to nitrogen, often referred to as the C:N ratio. Carbon-rich materials, often referred to as "browns," include things like dry leaves, straw, and newspaper. These materials provide structure to the compost pile and help create air pockets for oxygen flow. Nitrogen-rich materials, known as "greens," include kitchen scraps, grass clippings, and manure. These materials provide the necessary nutrients for microorganisms to break down the organic matter. A good rule of thumb is to aim for a C:N ratio of about 30 parts carbon to 1 part nitrogen. Experimenting with different materials and ratios can help you find the perfect balance for your compost pile and ultimately your garden.

Benefits of Composting

- **Reduces food waste:** Composting offers a sustainable solution to food waste by diverting food scraps from landfills.
  This practice not only reduces methane emissions into the
  environment but also alleviates the burden on our waste
  management systems.

- **Enhances soil health:** Compost will help out soil structure
  while also providing beneficial nutrients, which will give you
  more productive plants.

- **Saves money:** Giving your food scraps a second life by creating your fertilizer, virtually eliminates your need for the
  expensive store-bought options.

Choosing Your Composting Method

There are two main types of composting, each offering its unique
advantages.

- **Cold composting:** This is a slow method, taking a few
  months (sometimes up to a year) to produce the finished
  compost. It requires very little effort, though, and it works
  great for beginners and those with limited space. You just
  need alternating layers of green (food scraps or grass clippings) and brown (dry leaves, sticks, or shredded paper) materials. Make sure the pile stays moist and aerated by turning
  it occasionally. While this does take more time, it needs far
  less attention.

- **Hot composting:** This method will give you nutrient-rich compost much faster, typically within a few weeks, but it needs more active maintenance. Hot compost piles need a specific balance of green and brown materials, regular turning, and consistent moisture. For this method, your pile needs to maintain a consistent temperature between 140°F and 155°F. This temperature is ideal for killing off weeds and pathogens, but don't let it get much higher, as that can begin to kill the helpful bacteria and microorganisms. Again, this does take more effort, but it can be very beneficial for those who need soil amendments in a hurry or those who live in colder climates.

Factors to Consider Before Composting

Before you start your compost pile, a few factors need to be considered.

- **Your living situation:** If you have limited space, you may need to use a smaller bin or vermicomposting (composting worms).

- **Amount of organic waste:** If you have a lot of food scraps and yard waste, you might need to think of a larger composting system or start multiple piles.

- **Type of organic waste:** Yes, you will use yard waste and kitchen scraps, but you will need to avoid using meat, dairy products, and oily materials. These can negatively affect the decomposition process.

- **Time commitment:** If you don't have a lot of time to devote to your composting pile, cold composting is a great choice as it requires little time commitment. For those who have the time to do it, I would recommend using the hot composting method.

Composting Made Easy

The following are some essential steps to get you started with the composting part of your journey.

- **Gather your materials.** You want to gather everything together, then separate your kitchen scraps and yard waste. Try focusing on green materials like fruit and vegetable peels, eggshells, and coffee grounds. Then give the same focus to brown materials like dry leaves and shredded paper.

- **Choose your compost bin.** If you have a larger yard, you can designate a space for your material and build a small enclosure. However, that's not always feasible, so select a composting bin suitable for your space and needs. For smaller spaces, consider a lidded bin for odor control and easy turning. You can also use a compost tumbler, which will let your materials decompose faster.

- **Layer your materials.** Start your compost with a layer of brown material, then a layer of green materials. There are varying ratios out there, but the best place to start is with a 3:1 ratio of brown to green materials. It will make for optimal decomposition.

- **Maintain moisture and aeration:** Keep your pile moist. It should have the same moisture content as a damp sponge. To maintain aeration, regularly turn the pile with a shovel or compost turner. Turning the pile will ensure even decomposition.

- **Be patient.** Depending on your composting method and weather conditions, complete composting can take several months. Keep an eye on your pile. You may need to adjust material ratios or moisture levels as needed.

Mulching

We have discussed mulching a few times, but let's look into this simple yet highly effective gardening technique. With mulching, you cover the soil around your plants with a layer of material. This practice gives you a vast number of benefits for your plants and the overall health of your garden.

Understanding Mulch

Mulch is any material spread over the soil surface. It can be organic or inorganic material, and while it can seem like a purely aesthetic addition, mulching serves several key roles in your garden.

- **Moisture retention:** Mulch is much like a blanket on your soil, reducing water evaporation from the soil, which is particularly important during hot weather. It translates to less frequent watering on your end and much healthier plants.

- **Temperature regulation:** Again, like a blanket, mulch insulates the soil, which can regulate the extreme temperatures during the summer and winter months. It protects your roots from harmful fluctuations.

- **Weed suppression:** Mulch creates a physical barrier that hinders any weed seeds from germination and growth. Mulch will save you many labor hours of weed control.

- **Soil health improvement:** Organic mulch like wood chips or compost will decompose over time. This decomposition will put nutrients into the soil, and it will promote beneficial microbial activity.

Companion Planting and Mulch

By using cover crops, succession planting, or other companion planting techniques like the "three sisters," you can reduce garden maintenance. This is done because companion plants will act as a living mulch, suppressing weeds in your garden and retaining moisture, benefitting other plants in your garden.

Types of Mulch

As we've just learned, mulch can be broadly categorized into two types: organic and inorganic.

- **Organic mulch:** This can be anything from bark, wood chips, shredded leaves, compost, straw, grass clippings, or cover crops.

  - **Benefits:** Organic materials will gradually decompose, which will enrich the soil and further promote microbial life. It's also more aesthetically pleasing as it blends naturally with your garden.

- ○ **Drawbacks:** None of significance.

- **Inorganic mulch:** You will typically see this as stones, gravel, or landscape fabric. It's long-lasting and requires very little maintenance.

  - ○ **Benefits:** These materials are very effective in suppressing weeds, and they are the best choice for controlling erosion on slopes.

  - ○ **Drawbacks:** While there are benefits, inorganic mulch can cause issues in your garden. These materials don't decompose or add nutrients back to the soil. They can also trap heat and impact water infiltration, which means if you use these, you need to be strategic.

Organic mulch is preferred over inorganic mulch in natural gardening for several reasons. The gradual decomposition of organic mulch provides a slow-release fertilizer, supplying nutrients to plants steadily. Additionally, organic mulch improves soil structure, drainage, and aeration, resulting in healthier plants overall.

Creating and Applying Mulch

Making your own mulch is not only a cost-effective route, but it's sustainable, too. You can shred leaves, twigs, or any other waste from your garden by using a lawnmower or a shredder. Before you shred the material, though, ensure it is dry and free of weeds and diseases.

You should also double-check for any contaminant materials before applying the mulch to your garden.

When you are ready to apply your mulch, you should do the following.

1. **Clear the area:** Remove weeds, other existing vegetation, and other debris from around the base of your plants.

2. **Apply a layer of mulch.** Spread a layer of mulch around your plants. This layer needs to be around two to three inches and avoid placing it next to the stems to prevent rot.

3. **Replenish as needed:** As the mulch decomposes, it will thin out, so add a fresh layer periodically to maintain that two to three-inch depth.

Bonus Tip: Repurpose Your Banana Peels

Banana peels are rich in potassium and calcium, which make a great addition to your compost piles, but some gardeners even bury banana peels around plants like rose bushes or tomato plants for that boost of nutrients. Whether you choose to compost or try adding directly, using banana peels gives you a sustainable way to nourish your plants.

Pruning

Pruning is the strategic removal of plant parts, essential for garden maintenance. While often misunderstood as random cutting, pruning is a deliberate practice with specific techniques. It encourages healthy growth, maximizes yields, and improves harvest quality.

Benefits of Pruning

The following are just a few advantages that pruning can give you in your garden.

- **Improved airflow:** Thinning down some of the leaves will let more airflow around the plant. More airflow can also help prevent harmful fungal diseases.

- **Increased light penetration:** When you can thin out the foliage, sunlight can reach more parts of the plant, which encourages even growth and better fruit development.

- **Better fruiting quality:** When you direct your plant's energy toward fewer fruits, you are actually encouraging larger, healthier vegetables.

- **Encourages branching:** Pruning specific parts of a plant

can stimulate the plant to develop more productive branches.

- **Maintain plant shape:** This benefit is particularly important for your vining plants like tomatoes and cucumbers,
where controlling their growth improves manageability and
harvest efficiency.

Pruning Techniques

There are different types of pruning, and each of them is used for
specific purposes. Keep this in mind when you need to prune your
garden.

- **Pinching:** This is when you remove the growing tip of a
young plant, usually with your fingers. It promotes bushier
growth.

- **Suckering:** Suckering is the removal of non-fruiting shoots
that grow between the main stem and branches. It will happen in plants like tomatoes and eggplants.

- **Heading:** This is when you cut off the top portion of a stem
to encourage lower lateral growth. This method is commonly used for leafy green plants like lettuce.

- **Thinning:** The most common practice to remove unwanted stems, flowers, or fruits. It regulates spacing, which allows
for better light penetration and air circulation.

- **Topping:** When topping your plant, you remove the main
growing tip to control plant height. It will also encourage

branching. It is a great pruning method for vining plants like cucumbers and watermelons.

How to Prune

1. **Gather your tools:** Going back to your garden tool list from earlier, you need sharp, clean pruners or shears to ensure precise cuts.

2. **Identify what to prune:** When you research your plant, you will gain an understanding of its specific pruning needs. Consulting your resources will let you prune for optimal growth.

3. **Make clean cuts:** When you're ready to cut, you need to do this at a slight angle just above the leaf node or bud. It is where your new growth will emerge.

4. **Start small:** While you should be conservative with your cuts, this is especially true when the plant is young. Take time to observe your plant's response before further trimming.

5. **Sanitize your tools:** After you finish pruning, you need to disinfect your tools with rubbing alcohol or a bleach solution. It will prevent the spread of any plant diseases.

Harvesting

After weeks and months of planning, planting, amending, and nurturing, it's time to harvest your garden's vegetables. It is an absolutely
rewarding experience, whether it's your first harvest or if you're a
seasoned gardener. With the proper attention to detail, you can ensure
that your vegetables reach peak flavor and quality.

Harvesting Principles

- **Timing is key:** Most vegetables are best harvested during the
  cool morning hours, just after the dew dries. It is key because
  it ensures your harvest is crisp, cool, and hasn't been exposed
  to the harsh afternoon sun.

- **Sharp tools:** You have several options, from pruners and
  scissors to knives. Whatever tool you feel comfortable with
  should be sharp. Dull tools can damage the plant and affect
  regrowth, so always ensure that if your blades aren't sharp,
  sharpen them before use.

- **Selectivity:** Harvest your vegetables based on their maturity cues. Again, researching your plant (seed packets, online, or local growers) will let you know to look for cues like size, color, firmness, or days to maturity.

- **Handle with care:** Avoid bruising or damaging your vegetables during the harvest. This is why you need a sharp blade or pick them gently. After they are harvested, you need to put them in a cool, shady spot until you're ready to eat or preserve them.

Harvesting Certain Vegetables

We can look back at some of the plants we covered earlier to give you some examples of how to harvest your garden. Again, there may be slight differences among your plant varieties, so always double-check the harvesting procedures for your specific plant varieties.

- **Lettuce:** Harvest the outer leaves regularly to encourage new growth. You can use your scissors or gently snap off mature leaves with your fingers.

- **Spinach:** Much like lettuce, you will harvest individual leaves as needed. It will let the inner leaves continue growing.

- **Radishes:** You'll harvest radishes when their roots reach a desired size, usually between one to two inches in diameter. Be gentle as you pull them from the soil, as this protects the harvested plant and its neighbors.

- **Beets:** Beets are like radishes, except you'll wait until they are two to three inches in diameter. You can also harvest beet greens; just follow the same practice you would for spinach.

- **Kale:** Harvest individual leaves from the outer part of the plant. Again, this will allow the inner leaves to mature. Kale is a great freeze-tolerant crop, meaning you can harvest through the winter, especially if you are in a milder zone.

- **Swiss chard:** Harvest individual stalks by using a sharp knife to cut them at their base. Swiss chard is much like kale and can be harvested in the winter.

- **Carrots:** When carrots reach their desired thickness (one to two inches in diameter), they are ready to harvest. Use a garden fork to loosen the soil around them, then gently pull them out. Harvest carrots after the first frost for more sweetness.

- **Green beans:** Harvest green beans when they reach a firm, plump size (usually around four to six inches long). Snap them at the stem end, which will leave the plant intact for continued production.

- **Herbs:** You can harvest herbs throughout the growing season by pinching off individual leaves or stems. Keep in mind that regularly harvesting your herbs encourages bushier growth and promotes new leaf production.

Harvesting Tip

Harvest your tomatoes before peak blush and before rainfall. This will avoid tomato blossom rot and splitting. You can let them ripen on your counter.

***

Bonus Recipe: Tomato and Basil Burst Pasta

This simple yet delightful recipe captures the bright flavors of tomato and basil, a classic companion plant pairing, that will leave your taste buds smiling! The listed ingredients are just a starting point; feel free to experiment with your own versions by adding different herbs from your garden, more garlic, or extra olive oil to suit your taste.

Prep time: 5 min,

Cook time: 20 min,

Serves 2

Ingredients

4 TBS extra virgin olive oil

1 pint of cherry tomatoes

8 basil leaves, torn into small pieces

4 cloves garlic, crushed and chopped

2 servings of pasta (I like fusilli or penne)

2 TBS parmesan cheese topping

Salt to taste

Instructions

In a large pot, bring water to a boil and add the noodles. As the noodles cook, prepare the tomato and basil burst sauce. In a medium-sized pot add extra virgin olive oil and freshly harvested cherry tomatoes, and cook over medium heat. Once the tomatoes are hot, use the back of a wooden spoon to crush ¾ of them into a sauce. Leave some tomatoes whole. Add half of the torn basil and all the garlic. Cook on low heat and simmer for 20 minutes or longer. When the sauce is about ready, add the other half of the basil leaves to the sauce and cook for 5 min. Add salt to taste, serve tomato burst sauce over cooked and drained pasta, top with fresh basil and parmesan cheese, and serve with crusty bread. Enjoy the bright and beautiful flavors of your harvest!

***

Winter Cover Crops

When summer begins to fade the days get shorter and colder, and when you've harvested the last of your crops, you might feel the temptation to just leave your garden bare until it's time to start the process over the next year. However, you can give yourself a leg up in the next season by using a winter cover crop.

What Are Winter Cover Crops?

Winter cover crops are fast-growing plants sown in the late summer or early fall to protect and enrich your soil during the cold winter months. These are temporary residents, and they act as a living mulch. They will suppress weeds, prevent erosion, and they can fix nitrogen in the soil. When spring rolls around, they are either tilled under, mowed down, or allowed to decompose naturally. It adds organic matter and nutrients to enrich your soil for the new growing season.

Benefits of Winter Cover Crops

- **More fertile soil:** Winter cover crops, especially legumes like clover and peas, will fix nitrogen from the air, making it available to your spring crops. Additionally, when these crops are tilled under, their decomposing residues release vital nutrients and organic matter, which gives you healthy, fertile soil.

- **Reduced erosion:** Winter crops have an extensive root system, which helps hold soil particles in place. It reduces the erosion caused by wind and heavy rain, and it is crucial for sloping gardens or areas prone to heavy rainfall.

- **Weed suppression:** Cover crops are basically living mulch, which makes them effective at smothering weed seeds and preventing them from germinating. It reduces the need for herbicides and will leave you with a much cleaner garden bed in the spring.

- **Better soil structure:** The root systems not only hold soil particles together but also create channels for air and water to penetrate the soil, which promotes better drainage and aeration. It will lead to healthier plant growth later.

Main Types of Winter Cover Crops

There are two main types of winter cover crops, and they are based on their winter hardiness.

- **Winter-killed crops:** These are crops like oats, ryegrass, radishes, buckwheat, and turnips, and they are not winter-hardy. They will die out after the first frost; however, this isn't a bad thing. Their decomposing residues will provide many benefits to the soil.

- **Winter-hardy crops:** These are crops like rye, hairy vetch, Austrian winter peas, balansa clover, and crimson clover. They will survive through the winter and begin growing again in the spring. While they will resume growth, these crops are usually tilled under before planting your main season crops.

Planting Your Winter Cover Crop

Your location and climate will determine the ideal planting time for your winter crops. As a rule of thumb, I would aim to plant these around four to six weeks before your first frost is predicted to let the roots take hold in the soil. The following are just some basic steps to follow when sowing.

1. **Prepare the bed:** Clear the last of your summer crops and debris from the planting area and ensure that the top few inches of soil are loosened with a rake or hoe.

2. **Choose your crops:** Choose the plants best suited for your climate and soil conditions. Consider using a mix of different species for more benefits.

3. **Sow the seeds:** Spread the seeds evenly over the prepared bed, following the seeding rate on the seed packet. Lightly

rake the soil to cover the seed.

4. **Water:** Water as needed to make sure there is seed-to-soil contact that will lead to germination.

Making Your Harvest Timetable

Making your harvesting timetable will let you get the most out of your growing season. It's much like your planting calendar, which means it will take a little planning and double-checking. But that planning will lead you to a nearly year-round harvest of fresh vegetables.

Things to Consider for Your Timetable

- Consult your hardiness zone map. Different regions will have different growing seasons, and this map will help you understand your frost dates and average winter temperatures. It lets you know not just your planting window but your harvesting window as well.

- Choose the vegetables that will work with your region and your goals. Just because you want to grow something doesn't mean it will work in your region. And just because something can grow doesn't mean it's a plant you want. It should be a careful consideration.

- Plan your planting schedule. While your harvest timetable is important, your planting schedule takes precedence. This schedule should include your sowing and transplanting dates, and don't forget to factor in the germination period.

Building and Using Your Timetable

The timetable is fairly simple to make. You'll need to divide this into four columns (season, months, crops, and approximate planting dates). For your seasons, you can use five rows here, splitting your summer season into two sections. The following is only an example of that timetable. Remember to adapt and amend to make the table that works best for you and your garden.

Season	Crops	Approximate Planting Months	Approximate Harvesting Months
Spring	lettuce, spinach, kale radishes, peas, carrots, beets	February-March (indoors and from seeds)	March-May
Summer	tomatoes, peppers, eggplant, zucchini, squash, beans, corn	April-May (outdoors and from seedlings)	June-August
Summer (continued)	basil, parsley, cilantro, dill	May-June (outdoors, seeds)	July-August
Fall	broccoli, cauliflower, Brussels sprouts, Swiss chard, kale, pumpkins, winter squash	July-August (seeds and seedlings)	September-November
Winter	arugula, spinach, kale, lettuce (depends on climate)	September-October (seeds and seedlings)	December-February

Keep in mind that consistent maintenance throughout the year is essential to a healthy garden. Proper care through the growing season,

effective harvesting, and off-season care can lead to your garden producing vegetables at any season.

One final aspect to consider in your garden maintenance, crucial for
achieving a successful garden, is keeping your plants free from pests
and diseases.

Chapter Eight

Naturally Mitigate Pests and Diseases and Attract Beneficial Insects

Every summer, my neighbor would meticulously tend to his tomato plants, yet every year, those plants were attacked by swarms of fruit flies, and instead of vibrant foliage, the leaves of his plants were marred with black spots. Interestingly, my tomato plants, which were only a fence line apart, were producing bright red tomatoes alongside my fragrant basil bushes. There wasn't even a hint of the menacing fruit flies. I had healthy green leaves and plenty of ripe tomatoes.

It was such a stark contrast, and the only difference between our gardens was that I had implemented companion planting. Where his tomatoes stood alone in the battle against pests, mine benefited from the unyielding protection of the basil.

In this chapter, we will take a closer look into the world of pests and diseases, those unwanted, uninvited guests that can completely disrupt our gardening endeavors. We will unearth different strategies to identify garden foes, understand their impact on our plants, and discover how companion planting can be an extremely powerful tool in our natural pest control arsenal. This last chapter will help you create a garden ecosystem that provides you with maximum yield in your harvest and a healthy balance of life.

Common Garden Pests

While every gardener's pride and joy lies in a beautiful and bountiful garden, it is easily challenged by critters' love of the garden as well. Many of these critters are uninvited guests who consistently try, and often successfully, invade our gardens. These pests, which range from tiny insects to much larger rodents or mammals, wreak havoc on our plants. Their invasions impact plant growth, yield, and even livelihood. Effective defense mechanisms against common garden pests require proper identification of species and their habits.

- **Aphids:** These are small, soft-bodied insects with piercing mouths that suck sap from plant leaves and stems. It will cause stunted growth and yellowing or curled leaves. They reproduce quickly and leave behind honeydew, which is just a sticky residue that can be a breeding ground for sooty mold.

- **Whiteflies:** These are tiny, white, flying insects that also like to feed on plant sap, which causes similar damage to aphids. They will swarm when they're disturbed, and like aphids, they leave honeydew behind.

- **Tomato hornworms:** If you see large green caterpillars with horn-like protrusions on their backs, those are tomato horn-worms. They are the larvae of the sphinx moth, and they chomp through the foliage and fruits of your tomato plants and leave large holes.

- **Slugs and snails:** Slimy, soft-bodied mollusks like these two leave a glistening trail on the leaves, flowers, and fruits they eat. They thrive in moist environments and cause significant damage. Slugs and snails are especially a threat to seedlings and young plants.

Aphids   Whiteflies

Tomato Hornworm   Snail

Natural, Affordable Pest Control Solutions

You don't need to turn to harmful pesticides to eliminate these threats. Commercial pesticides can be deadly to beneficial insects and pollinators, but fortunately, many natural and affordable solutions exist to combat these pests. The following are just a few of those methods.

- **Peppermint castile soap spray:** This option is readily available and earth-friendly, and it will repel various garden pests like aphids, whiteflies, and some other insects. All you need to do is mix a tablespoon of castile soap with a liter of water and spray the mix directly onto the affected plants.

- **Garlic and cayenne pepper spray:** It's a spicy mix, but it will deter a wide range of pests because of its strong odor and taste. Take a tablespoon of cayenne pepper powder, one crushed garlic clove, and one liter of water; then let the ingredients steep for 24 hours. Strain the mix, add it to your spray bottle, and spray it on the affected plants.

- **Beer traps:** Slugs and snails simply can't resist the smell of beer. Take a shallow container and bury it level with your soil surface. You'll add beer to the container, and these pests will crawl in and not be able to escape.

- **Organic insect oil:** Derived from plants like neem or cottonseed, organic oils will smother and disrupt the development of various pests like aphids, mites, and mealybugs.

- **Eggshell powder:** This is a readily available, cost-effective solution, and it will act as a physical barrier against pests like beetles and slugs. All you need to do is crush eggshells into a fine powder, then sprinkle them on the leaves where there are pests or directly onto the soil. The sharp edges of the shells deter and kill pests, and as the shell breaks down, it will provide your soil with a small shot of calcium.

Companion Planting for Natural Pest and Disease Control

As we learned earlier in this book, companion planting is a great strategy that uses the beneficial relationships between plants to deter pests while attracting beneficial insects like ladybugs and lacewings. But let's look again at some of the most common examples of companion planting and how they work.

- **Basil and tomatoes:** The strong scent of basil will repel flies, mosquitoes, and even the hungry tomato hornworms, who are after your tomato plants.

- **Sage and cabbage:** Sage releases a strong scent that will deter cabbage moths and cabbage loopers, which will wreak havoc on any of your *Brassicaceae* family vegetables.

- **Beans and marigolds:** Marigolds have vibrant orange and yellow blooms that add beauty to any garden, but they also deter pests like aphids, whiteflies, and nematodes that can harm the bean plants.

- **Celery and cauliflower:** Celery will act as a trap crop for aphids, which attracts them away from the more delicate cauliflower plants. When the celery becomes infested, you can remove the plant and dispose of the pests.

- **Cucumber and corn:** Although corn isn't a direct pest repellent, the tall stalks provide welcome shade for cucumbers, which will keep them cool and resistant to powdery mildew.

- **Radish and cucumber:** Radishes have a pungent smell that can deter cucumber beetles. Also, the cucumbers can provide some shade for the radishes, making this a beneficial pairing for both plants.

- **Beans and eggplant:** Beans will fix nitrogen in the soil, which benefits eggplants, while the bean plant's foliage will help shade the eggplant and deter flea beetles.

- **Parsley and carrot:** The strong aroma of parsley can repel root flies, which will protect your carrots from underground damage.

- **Nasturtiums and squash:** Nasturtiums will act as a trap crop for aphids, attracting them away from squash plants. Their vibrant flowers also attract insects like ladybugs, which are natural predators of aphids.

- **Garlic and tomatoes:** The strong odor of garlic can repel aphids, tomato hornworms, and even whiteflies, creating a protective barrier for your tomatoes.

- **Oregano and broccoli:** Oregano will attract hoverflies, which are also natural predators of the aphids found on broccoli plants.

- **Thyme and *brassicas*:** The scent of thyme will repel cabbage moths and other pests that target your *brassica* plants, like broccoli and kale.

- **Thyme and lettuce:** Interplanting thyme with lettuce will deter whiteflies and other flying insects.

Other Tips for Pest Control

- **Sprinkle cayenne pepper:** Lightly dust cayenne pepper around the base of your plants. It can deter pests like beetles and slugs. Just remember to reapply after a heavy rain or watering.

- **Use vegetable oil:** Soak a cotton swab in vegetable oil and dab it on individual insects like aphids, whiteflies, and beetles. The oil will suffocate the pests without hurting the plants. It is a good idea for a few insects but not for larger infestations.

While there are solutions to pest problems, prevention is a key component here. Maintaining a healthy garden environment with proper watering, fertilization, and sanitation will go a long way in making sure that pests don't move in. By combining these strategies, though, you will ensure that you have a pest-resistant garden.

Disease Prevention and Management

Just like us humans, plants are prone to a variety of ailments. Plant diseases are caused by different factors like fungi, bacteria, viruses, and unfavorable environmental conditions. This is why recognizing the signs and symptoms of common plant diseases is crucial. It allows you to take prompt action and safeguard your garden's overall health. So, let's look at some of those common garden ailments and ways that you can manage them.

Powdery Mildew:

This is a disease that is easily recognizable by its "powdery" look. Often white or gray will affect your plants' leaves, stems, and flowers. This mildew will appear in cool, humid conditions.

- **Plants affected:** The cucurbit family includes squash, pumpkins, melons, and cucumbers. The nightshade family consists of tomatoes, eggplant, and peppers. Roses and legumes are also important groups to consider.

- **Treatment:** Apply a mixture of baking soda and water or neem oil diluted in water. Spray the tops and undersides of the leaves.

- **Prevention:** Prune and ensure that there is enough air circulation. It includes making sure you have enough space between plants. Also, avoid overhead watering techniques, as moisture will promote fungal growth.

Downy Mildew:

Unlike the powder variety, this fungal disease will appear as brown or yellow spots on the undersides of leaves with a fuzzy growth on the tops. It can eventually curl the leaves or cause them to drop.

- **Plants affected:** Basil and nearly all common cucurbits such as watermelon, zucchini, winter squashes, cucumbers, and pumpkins are commonly affected plants. Grapes, soybeans, spinach, and sunflowers are also among the targets.

- **Treatment:** Use the same mixture option that you chose for powdery mildew, except focus the spray on just the underside of the leaves.

- **Prevention:** Water the plants at ground level to avoid wetting the leaves. Choosing disease-resistant varieties can also help in prevention.

Black Spot:

You will typically find this fungal disease in your roses. You can spot this by the dark spots on the leaves and stems of your plants. Don't dismiss them if they are small. While they can start out that way, they will get bigger and merge with other spots, causing your plant to lose its leaves and become weaker overall.

- **Plants affected:** Rose bushes, citrus trees like lemon, orange, and grapefruit, as well as apple and pear trees, mango trees, and grapevines, are all included.

- **Treatment:** Prune the affected leaves and stems and use a fungicide with potassium bicarbonate or neem oil.

- **Prevention:** Maintain optimal air circulation, water at the base of the plant (avoid overhead watering), and choose disease-resistant varieties.

Blossom End Rot:

Vine-growing and flowering vegetables, such as tomatoes, peppers, eggplants, and zucchini, are susceptible to blossom end rot, a condition caused by calcium and water deficiency during fruit maturation. Symptoms include light brown spots at the bottom of the fruit, which darken, develop craters, and eventually lead to fruit rot.

- **Plants affected:** Flowering vegetables like tomatoes, peppers, eggplants, and zucchini.

- **Treatment:** Remove affected fruits, adjusting watering to prevent drying out (while avoiding over-watering to prevent splitting), and adding mulch to maintain soil moisture at the base of plants.

- **Prevention:** Use well-draining soil enriched with organic material and nutrients like compost and peat moss to aid calcium uptake by roots. Additionally, test soil pH levels to ensure they are around 6.5 for optimal prevention of this condition.

Mosaic Virus:

Mosaic viruses can impact over 150 types of plants, including various fruits, vegetables, and flowers. This disease causes leaves to develop a discolored pattern ranging between streaks of yellow, white, and dark green spots on the leaves. This disease stunts plant growth inhibiting yields.

- **Plants affected:** Commonly affected plants include tomatoes, squashes, cauliflower, and cucumbers, but many others can be susceptible.

- **Treatment:** Unfortunately, a viral infection has no cure, which means you need to remove and destroy the infected plants to prevent the virus from spreading.

- **Prevention:** Practicing good hygiene is one effective measure, so make sure you disinfect your tools after handling infected plants. Also, practice insect control measures to deter aphids and other critters that carry the virus.

Damping-off Disease:

Primarily affecting seedlings, this fungal disease causes plants to rot and die shortly after germination.

- **Plants affected:** Many vegetable and fruit seeds are susceptible.

- **Treatment:** Infected seedlings are lost; therefore, remove and destroy them to prevent the disease from spreading.

- **Prevention:** Your seed starting mix and containers need to be sterilized, and don't forget to thin seedlings to provide better air circulation. Also, don't overwater your seedlings

Fusarium Wilt:

Fusarium wilt is a fungal disease that lives in your soil and will attack the vascular system of your plants. It will cause wilting, yellowing, and, eventually, the death of your plants.

- **Plants affected:** Tomatoes, peppers, eggplants, cucurbits, beans, and cabbages can commonly be affected by the fungus.

- **Treatment:** There is nothing effective to treat established infections; therefore, the removal and destruction of affected plants will stop further spread.

- **Prevention:** Maintain good soil drainage and health, choose disease-resistant plants, and practice crop rotation.

Verticillium Wilt:

This disease is similar to Fusarium wilt, attacking the vascular system of your plants. It causes wilting, stunted growth, and eventually death.

- **Plants affected:** Tomatoes, potatoes, peppers, eggplants, cucumbers, and strawberries.

- **Treatment:** Again, like Fusarium wilt, there is no effective treatment; you will need to remove and destroy infected plants.

- **Prevention:** Preventative measures are the same as Fusarium wilt: maintain soil drainage, use disease-resistant types, and practice crop rotation.

Sooty Mold:

Sooty mold is a black, fungus-like growth that doesn't directly harm your plants, but it does love the honeydew left behind by sap-sucking insects like aphids.

- **Plants affected:** Many vegetable and fruit plants are affected, especially those that have fuzzy leaves like squash and melons because they can trap water and dust that provides the food for mold growth.

- **Treatment:** Use the measures we went over earlier to rid yourself of your insect problem, which will eliminate the food source for the mold. After you've handled your bug issues, you can use insecticidal soap or neem oil to remove the mold.

- **Prevention:** Monitor your plants to look for signs of insect infestations and handle them promptly. Avoid watering the leaves and direct water towards the soil and roots of the plant.

Snow Mold:

Snow mold is a common fungal disease that typically affects grasses during cool weather and heavy moisture. It will show up as cotton-like patches as the snow melts during the early spring.

- **Plants affected:** Cool-season (winter) crops like ryegrass and fescue.

- **Treatment:** Rake the affected areas to take out the fungal mat and enhance air circulation.

- **Prevention:** Make sure your garden has good air circulation and proper moisture drainage. You can even opt to use a fungicide-preventative in the late fall or early spring.

Rust:

You'll spot this fungal disease as it manifests as orange, red, or brown pustules on plant leaves and stems. It can eventually lead to defoliation and the overall weakening of the plant.

- **Plants affected:** Rust can develop on summer flowering plants including squash and melons, rose bushes, sunflowers, and sweetpeas.

- **Treatment:** Remove and destroy the infected plant parts (not the whole plant). Apply a fungicide that contains sulfur or copper.

- **Prevention:** Water at ground level (not overhead), and give your plants adequate spacing for air circulation. Also, choose resistant plant varieties.

The Power of Companion Planting in Disease Prevention

Diseases need specific treatment strategies, like removing and destroying plant parts or whole plants. However, companion planting can play a role in reducing the overall impact of plant diseases. So, what can companion planting offer in the way of disease prevention?

- **Improved soil quality:** Companion plants with deep root systems will help improve aeration and drainage. It can significantly reduce the risk of moisture-related diseases like fungal infections and damping-off. Additionally, by using legumes, you will fix the nitrogen levels in the soil, enriching it with nutrients that promote plant health and make your plants resistant to disease.

- **Pest control:** By bringing in beneficial insects like ladybugs and lacewings, companion plants can naturally deter pests that spread certain diseases.

Of course, always remember that prevention is key. While you can't guarantee complete success in getting rid of diseases, you can significantly reduce the risk.

Understanding Beneficial Insects

Your garden is a bustling ecosystem, which means that not every insect you see is out to harm your garden. Many of them are beneficial, playing vital roles in maintaining a healthy and productive garden. So, let's take a look at some of these helpful critters and how they assist a successful garden.

- **Soldier beetle:** These beetles are brightly colored, but it's their larvae that benefit your garden, as they eliminate pests like aphids, caterpillars, and grubs.

- **Big-eyed bug:** You'll find these nocturnal insects feasting on moth larvae, which includes the highly destructive cutworm.

- **Hoverfly:** They are often mistaken for wasps, but these beneficial bugs hover near flowers, which makes them key pollinators. Their larvae are ferocious predators of aphids and other tiny insects.

- **Ladybugs:** These are a revered friend of gardens everywhere. Ladybugs and their larvae are constantly feeding and consuming large quantities of aphids, mealybugs, and scale insects.

- **Rough stink bug:** You can't miss their pungent odor, but these insects are predators of caterpillars and other garden pests.

- **Lacewing:** These delicate insects and their larvae, known as aphid lions, are fierce aphid hunters, eating hundreds of pests through their lifecycle.

- **Dragonfly and damselfly:** You'll find these aerial hunters patrolling the sky, ready to snatch flies, mosquitos, and other flying insects.

- **Braconid wasp:** These tiny wasps will become parasites to various pests. They lay their eggs within their host's body, eventually leading to the death of that insect.

- **Bees:** You'll likely have a diverse array of bees in your region. These pollinators are essential for a flowering plant's reproduction, so you need them for your fruits and vegetables.

- **Butterflies:** Like the native bees, you'll have an array of butterflies vital in pollination. They will ensure the development of fruits, seeds, and flowers.

- **Spiders:** Despite causing a fright for some gardeners, these web-weaving predators capture a myriad of insects, which controls pest populations.

- **Praying mantis:** This insect waits for its prey to come within reach before attacking. They are great at controlling grasshoppers, crickets, and other larger insects.

Attracting Beneficial Insects

Creating a habitat that is welcoming to beneficial insects is key to maintaining a healthy garden ecosystem. The following are some of the plants that will attract helpful critters.

- **Aromatic herbs:** Using herbs like lavender, thyme, rosemary, and oregano helps attract a variety of beneficial insects like hoverflies, butterflies, and lacewings.

- **Marigolds:** These colorful flowers can repel certain pests, and they can attract hoverflies and parasitic wasps. You should note that marigolds can deter other pollinators, so be careful or avoid placing them next to vegetables and other flowering plants that rely on pollination.

- **Nasturtiums:** These gorgeous blooms attract bugs like ladybugs and hoverflies, and they can be a great trap crop for aphids, drawing them away from your other plants.

- **Cosmos:** These flowers are airy and great at attracting butterflies, allowing them to pollinate any of your fruiting plants.

- **Zinnias:** These vibrant flowers attract butterflies, bees, and other pollinators, and they add a great touch of color to any garden.

- **Sunflowers:** These towering flowers will also attract several insects like bees, butterflies, and ladybugs.

- **Dill:** This fragrant herb will deter some harmful insects while also attracting hoverflies, parasitic wasps, and ladybugs.

- **Parsley:** Much like dill, parsley attracts various beneficial insects, like butterflies and hoverflies.

Garden Fencing

A well-constructed garden fence will have a myriad of benefits. It can enhance the beauty, functionality, and security of your plot. Not only will it give you a visually pleasing border, but it will also deter the other unwanted visitors that are attracted to your garden, be it the two-legged visitors or the furry ones.

Benefits of Garden Fencing

- **Security:** A fence will create a physical barrier that deters trespassers and other intruders from your property. This is quite important if your garden is near a public space or if you have anything valuable stored outside.

- **Protection from wildlife:** Deer, rabbits, raccoons, and other animals can be a very destructive force to your carefully cultivated garden. A fence will work to keep these critters out, making sure your plants meet their full potential.

- **Privacy:** A taller fence can give you a feeling of seclusion and privacy, which will allow you to see your garden as a retreat. It can also provide a shady zone for your plants.

- **Enhanced aesthetics:** Fences have many varieties of styles and materials, and they are a great addition to the overall design of your garden. You can frame a specific area or simply make a designated space.

- **Support for climbing plants:** Certain fences, like trellises or latticework, give support for your climbing plants, which gives you yet another layer of visual appeal and an additional layer of privacy.

- **Defines boundaries:** A fence will clearly mark the perimeter of your garden, which can prevent misunderstandings with your neighbors.

Creating a Garden Fence

While building a fence can seem like a steep task, it can be a rewarding DIY project. All you need is some careful planning for good execution. The following is a general outline of what you need to do.

- **Planning and Design**

  ○ **Measure your area.** It will determine the exact perimeter of the space you want to fence.

  ○ **Choose your materials.** Look for fencing materials that suit your budget and aesthetic preference. Ensure that it's a sturdy material. The most common options are wood, metal, vinyl, and composite materials.

  ○ **Check local building codes.** Make sure your fence complies with local building codes or restrictions regarding height, materials, and placement.

- **Preparation**

  ○ **Mark the fence line.** Use stakes and string to mark where your fence will go.

  ○ **Locate your utility lines.** Before you make your first dig, contact your local utility locating service to mark all underground lines. It will help you avoid any accidental damage or injury.

- **Building the Fence**

  ○ Follow any instructions that come with your chosen fencing material. These instructions will usually involve how to set posts, attach panels, and possibly construct the gate.

- **Finishing Touches**

  ○ When you have your fence built, apply all necessary finishing touches like paint, stain, hardware, or decorative elements.

Cost-Saving Tips

- **Use repurposed materials.** As long as they fit your local building codes, explore second-hand stores, online marketplaces, and other places to find used or recycled fencing materials. You might be able to find salvaged wood, metal panels, or even bricks that can be used in your fence design, and they will be far cheaper than buying them brand new.

- **Choose DIY over professional installation.** While you can get a high-quality, error-free job done by a professional fencing crew, it can be very pricey. Building the fence yourself can greatly reduce costs, especially if you opt for pre-fabricated panels or simplistic designs.

- **Compare prices:** Shop around and get quotes from different suppliers for materials and tools before making any purchases.

Pests and Deterrent Plant Chart

For this first chart, we will use the most common pests you will find in your garden and the plants that can act as deterrents. When planning your garden design, you can expand on this with pests and plants native to your area.

Pests	Deterrent Plants
Aphids	Lavender, marigolds, mint, nasturtiums
Cabbage moths	Catnip, rosemary
Japanese beetles	Garlic, mint, tansy
Mosquitos	Basil, catnip, citronella, lavender
Slugs and snails	While not plant deterrents, you can use beer traps, coffee grounds, or eggshells.

Beneficial Insects and Attractive Plants

Much like the chart above, when you plan your garden, look for the beneficial bugs and the plants that will attract them that are native to your region.

Beneficial Insects	Attractive Plants
Ladybugs, lacewings, hoverflies	Dill, fennel, yarrow
Braconid wasps	Borage, cilantro, dill
Parasitic wasps	Dill, fennel, yarrow
Dragonflies	Lavender, mint, yarrow,

ele

This chapter took us through the world of garden pests and diseases, highlighting the importance of proactive measures to ensure every harvest is healthy and bountiful. While we can't avoid every visitor to the garden, when we create a balanced ecosystem and foster beneficial partnerships, it goes a long way in mitigating unwanted pests.

Remember that prevention is key. Taking care of your plants and soil and even incorporating companion planting in your garden will go a long way in keeping pests out. And while prevention can help you, being vigilant is the next step. Regularly monitor your plants for any signs of trouble, like holes in your leaves, discoloration, wilting, or signs of disease. When you catch something early, you can act promptly, preventing the problem from escalating to your entire garden. Remember, this takes dedication, proactive measures, and an understanding of the natural environment around you.

***

Fellow plant enthusiasts,

As you wrap up *The Complete Beginner's Guide to Companion Planting*, I hope you've found it as enjoyable and informative as I have in creating it! Are you feeling inspired to put your new knowledge into action and grow a bountiful garden? If so, why not share your excitement and insights with others by leaving a review?

Your review can help more gardening enthusiasts discover the value of this book and the joys of companion planting. It's not just about sharing your thoughts; it's about helping others experience the same joy and fulfillment that you've found in your garden. Imagine the impact you could have on someone else's gardening journey by sharing your experience!

So, before you move on to your next gardening adventure, take a few moments to leave your review. It's simple! Just scan the QR code or go online to where you purchased the book and click the "Write a Review" button. Share your thoughts, and you're done!

Let's spread the joy of companion planting together!

Conclusion

In our journey through companion planting, we've uncovered the captivating world of plant partnerships and explored techniques for cultivating a flourishing, sustainable garden. You've discovered how plants collaborate, attracting beneficial insects while deterring pests and diseases, and even enhancing the growth of neighboring plants.

What struck me most when I started learning about companion planting was that it's more than just planting specific combinations; it's about embracing a holistic approach to your garden's ecosystem. Understanding the intricate relationships between plants and their environment allows you to create a harmonious and sustainable garden.

You've also learned the importance of consistent care and maintenance. Regularly tending to your plants, ensuring they have enough water and sunlight, and maintaining healthy soil are crucial for success. By incorporating these practices into your routine, you're not only benefiting your garden but also the planet.

Companion planting promotes natural pest control, reducing the need for pesticides. Using organic materials and composting also reduces the reliance on synthetic fertilizers, ultimately cutting down on greenhouse gas emissions. It's about playing a small part in creating a more sustainable future.

One story from this book illustrates the transformative power of companion planting. Our gardener initially struggled but was inspired to try companion planting after learning about it from her local garden center. Despite initial skepticism, she gave it a shot, and her garden flourished. Not only did she enjoy a bountiful harvest, but she also supported local bee populations, benefiting the environment.

Armed with this knowledge and guided by sustainability principles, you now have the tools to create your own thriving garden. So, experiment, take risks, and have fun! Every seed you plant, every weed you pull, and every harvest you enjoy is a reason to celebrate. You're not just connecting with nature; you're helping create a healthier, more sustainable planet.

As you find success in your garden, share your knowledge with others. Whether helping neighbors start their gardens or leaving a book review, your insights can inspire others to embrace companion planting and sustainable gardening practices.

References

Abid, A. K. (2023, March 17). *10 unusual gardening tips that actually work*. IndiaTimes. https://www.indiatimes.com/lifestyle/gardeni ng/10-unusual-gardening-tips-596174.html

Albert, S. (2022, May 9). *Companion planting vegetables and pollinator plants*. Gardeningknowhow. https://www.gardeningknowho w.com/garden-how-to/beneficial/pollinator-companions.htm

Amy. (2021, March 12). *How to decide where to put your garden*. Gardens That Matter. https://gardensthatmatter.com/choose-garde n-location/

Andrews (MA), U. of S. (2021, March 12). *Flowers I like to companion plant with vegetables*. Treehugger. https://www.treehugger.com/f lowers-companion-plant-vegetable-garden-5115902

Aristizabal, M. C. (2023, January 31). *Companion planting or how to get the most out of your micro garden!* Earth Day. https://earthday.ca/2023/01/31/companion-planting-or-h ow-to-get-the-most-out-of-your-micro-garden/

Baley, A. (2018, April 5). *Benefits of cinnamon on plants: Using cinnamon for pests, cuttings, & fungicide*. Gardening Know How. https://www.gardeningknowhow.com/garden-how-to/inf o/using-cinnamon-on-plants.htm

BCC Gardeners' World Magazine. (2022, May 12). *20 money-saving tips for gardeners*. BBC Gardeners World Magazine. https://www.gardenersworld.com/how-to/grow-plants/20 -money-saving-tips-for-gardeners/

Benefits of organic gardening | why garden organically? (n.d.) . Safer® Brand. https://www.saferbrand.com/advice/organic-gar dening/why-organic

Boeckmann, C. (2022, May 26). *Companion planting guide for vegetables*. Almanac. https://www.almanac.com/companion-plantin g-guide-vegetables

Boeckmann, C. (2024a, January 18). *Tips for transplanting seedlings*. Old Farmer's Almanac. https://www.almanac.com/tips-transpla nting-seedlings

Boeckmann, C. (2024b, February 16). *Companion vegetable garden layout*. Www.almanac.com . https://www.almanac.com/planning-companion-planting-gard en#:~:text=Also%2C%20many%20flowers%20make%20ideal

Boeckmann, C. (2024c, February 16). *Raised bed garden layout plans*. Www.almanac.com. https://www.almanac.com/raised-bed-veget able-garden-layouts-beginners

Boeckmann, C. (2024d, February 29). *Where to put a vegetable garden*. Almanac.com. https://www.almanac.com/where-put-veget able-garden

Boeckmann, C. (2024e, March 4). *Soil preparation: How do you prepare garden soil for planting?* Almanac.com. https://www.almana c.com/soil-preparation-how-do-you-prepare-garden-soil-planting

Bondareva, L. et. al. (2021, September 26). *Pesticides: Behavior in Agricultural Soil Plants*. Molecules MDPI. https://www.ncbi.nl m.nih.gov/pmc/articles/PMC8434383/

Boughton. (2019). *Soil types*. Boughton. https://www.boughton.co
.uk/products/topsoils/soil-types/

Carla. (2017, September 19). *Organic edible gardens with gaia's organic gardens*. Gaias Organic Gardens. https://www.gaiasorganic
gardens.com.au/companion-planting-guide/

Carlson, S. (2018, April 18). *What's the best
type of soil for plants?* Blog.petersoncompanies.net
. https://blog.petersoncompanies.net/best-type-of-soil-for-plant
s#:~:text=Best%20Soil%20For%20Plants%2C%20Loam

Casley, N. (2021, March 30). *5 common watering mistakes
you are probably making*. Bokashi Living | Bokashi Ex-
perts. https://bokashiliving.com/5-common-watering-mistakes
-you-are-probably-making/

Chadwick, P. (2020, October). *Guidelines for
harvesting vegetables*. Piedmontmastergardeners.org
. https://piedmontmastergardeners.org/article/guidelines-for-ha
rvesting-vegetables/#:~:text=The%20best%20time%20of%20day

Charbonneau, J. (2017, April 13). *7 benefits of companion planting*.
Southern Exposure. https://blog.southernexposure.com/2017/0
4/7-benefits-of-companion-planting/

Chesley, A. (2022, May 16). *How to use triangular spacing to fit more
plants*. Salt in My Coffee. https://saltinmycoffee.com/how-to-use
-triangular-plant-spacing/

Companion planting chart. (2014, August 15). Growin Crazy Acres.
https://growincrazyacres.com/companion-planting-chart/

Companion planting chart - garden with companion plants. (2012, July
5). Smiling Gardener. https://www.smilinggardener.com/organi
c-vegetable-gardening/companion-planting-chart/

Companion planting what plants grow best together. (n.d.). Finch +
Folly. https://www.finchandfolly.com/companion-planting

Copeland, B. (2023, June 26). *10 easy vegetables you don't need a green thumb to grow.* Martha Stewart. https://www.marthastewart.com /easiest-vegetables-to-grow-in-garden-7553381

Dr. Samanthi. (2018, April 11). *Difference between hydrophytes mesophytes and xerophytes.* Compare the Difference between Similar Terms. https://www.differencebetween.com/difference-betwe en-hydrophytes-and-vs-mesophytes-and-vs-xerophytes/

Drew, S. (2023, October 19). *Companion planting: Facts & myths.* Bite Sized Gardening. https://www.bitesizedgardening.co.uk/co mpanion-planting-facts-myths/how-to-dig-for-victory/

Dyer, M. H. (2017, April 25). *Zone 9 planting guide: When to plant vegetables in zone 9 gardens.* Gardeningknowhow. https://www.gardeningknowhow.com/garden-how-to/gardening -by-zone/zone-9-10-11/zone-9-vegetable-planting-guide.htm

Feaster, F. (n.d.). *44 common garden pests.* HGTV. https://www.hgtv.com/outdoors/landscaping-and-hard scaping/16-common-garden-pests-pictures

Fetrow, C. (2022, June 13). *Companion planting for the modern gardener.* Lancaster Farming. https://www.lancasterfarming.com/country-life/gardening/comp anion-planting-for-the-modern-gardener/article_ffce870c-eb1e-1 1ec-b724-cfdfdde26c8c.html

Find your growing zone √ USDA zone map √ planting zones √ growing zone. (n.d.). Grow Organic. https://www.groworganic.com/page s/what-is-my-growing-zone

5 benefits of growing from seed. (n.d.). Www.bountifulgardener.com . https://www.bountifulgardener.com/5-benefits-of-growing-fro m-seed/

5 reasons to grow organic vegetables. (2021, April 1). Earths Ally. https://earthsally.com/gardening-basics/5-reasons-to-grow-organi

c-vegetables.html#:~:text=Organic%20gardening%20doesn%27t%
20rely

Flowers that deter pest insects from your vegetable garden. (n.d.). The
Grounds Guys. https://www.groundsguys.com/blog/2022/febr
uary/flowers-that-deter-pest-insects-from-your-vegeta/

Forney, J. (n.d.). *How to save a drowning plant.*
HGTV. https://www.hgtv.com/outdoors/flowers-and-plants/ho
useplants/2019/how-to-save-a-drowning-plant

Fowler, H. (2013, March 13). *Gardening for dum-
mies: Companion planting.* Onecreativemommy.com
. https://onecreativemommy.com/planning-the-garden-compani
on-planting-free-printable-helpful-insects/

Gao, J., & Zhang, F. (2023). Influence of Companion Planting on
Microbial Compositions and Their Symbiotic Network in Pepper
Continuous Cropping Soil. *Journal of Microbiology and Biotech-
nology, 33*(6), 760–770. https://doi.org/10.4014/jmb.2211.11032

Garden soil: How to prepare soil for planting. (n.d.). Grabco. https://
www.grabco.co.uk/garden-soil-preparation-guide/

Gardeners Supply Company. (2019). *How to start seeds - germinating
seeds.* Gardeners Supply. https://www.gardeners.com/how-to/ho
w-to-start-seeds/5062.html

Gardening in zones 7, 8, 9 or 10. (n.d.). Www.gardeners.com
. https://www.gardeners.com/how-to/gardening-zones-7-10/72
19.html#:~:text=Zone%207

Gilmour. (2019, April 4). *Planting zones map - find your plant hardiness growing zone.* Gilmour. https://gilmour.com/planting-zones
-hardiness-map

Grant, A. (2017, January 12). *Zone 5 vegetables –
when to plant zone 5 vegetable gardens.* Gardening-

knowhow. https://www.gardeningknowhow.com/garden-how-t
o/gardening-by-zone/zone-5/zone-5-vegetable-gardens.htm

Grant, A. (2022, May 12). *Companion planting for carrots.*
G a r d e n i n g k n o w h o w .
https://www.gardeningknowhow.com/edible/vegetables/carrot/c
arrot-companions.htm#:~:text=Carrot%20Companion%20Plants

Grant, A. (2023, February 17). *Guide to zone 3 vegetable gardening - tips on vegetable gardening in zone 3.* Gardening Know
How. https://www.gardeningknowhow.com/garden-how-to/gar
dening-by-zone/zone-3/zone-3-vegetables.htm

Grant, B. (2023, June 6). *Zone 1 plants: Cold hardy
plants for zone 1 gardening.* Www.gardeningknowhow.com
. https://www.gardeningknowhow.com/garden-how-to/gardeni
ng-by-zone/zone-1-2/zone-1-gardening.htm

Grant, J. (2020a, September 5). *Zone 1 planting guide.* Garden Tow-
er. https://www.gardentowerproject.com/blogs/learning-center/
zone-1-planting-guide

Grant, J. (2020b, September 5). *Zone 2 planting guide.* Garden Tow-
er. https://www.gardentowerproject.com/blogs/learning-center/
zone-2-planting-guide

Growing zones guide: Zone 4. (2021). FastGrowingTrees.com
. https://www.fast-growing-trees.com/pages/growing-zones-guid
e-zone-4#:~:text=Cold%20weather%20doesn%27t%20have

Guide to garden watering methods. (n.d.). Miraclegro.com
. https://miraclegro.com/en-us/projects-planning/guide-to-garde
n-watering-methods.html

Hagen, L. (2019). *12 gardening tools to buy - essentials for beginners.*
Garden Design. https://www.gardendesign.com/how-to/tools.h
tml

Hailey, L. (2023, September 6). *Companion planting gone wrong: 21 planting combinations to avoid*. Epic Gardening. https://www.epicgardening.com/plant-combinations-to-avoid/

Halleck, L. F. (2022, February). *Managing great expectations*. Gardencentermag.com. https://www.gardencentermag.com/article/managing-great-expectations/

Hardiness zone 2 - the best plants to grow in your garden. (n.d.). Gardenia.net. https://www.gardenia.net/plants/hardiness-zones/2

Harvest chart. (n.d.). PROingredients. https://www.proingredients.com/harvest-chart/

Hassani, N. (2021, November 29). *The basics of companion planting garden crops*. The Spruce. https://www.thespruce.com/companion-planting-with-chart-5025124

Hayes, B. (2021a, March 13). *Block planting: A simple gardening technique to grow more veggies*. Morning Chores. https://morningchores.com/block-planting/

Hayes, B. (2021b, November 28). *9 green bean companion plants to consider*. Gardening Channel. https://www.gardeningchannel.com/green-bean-companion-plants/

Herman, F. (2021, November 24). *All you need to know about irrigation to grow in dry seasons*. Futurepump. https://futurepump.com/irrigation-to-grow-in-the-dry-season/

Hicks-Hamblin, K. (2021, September 29). *The benefits of companion planting*. Gardener's Path. https://gardenerspath.com/how-to/organic/benefits-companion-planting/

How earthworms can help your soil. (2021). Www.dpi.nsw.gov.au. https://www.dpi.nsw.gov.au/agriculture/soils/guides/soil-biology/earthworms#:~:text=Benefits%20of%20earthworms

How much should I water my plant? (n.d.). Www.patchplants.com . https://www.patchplants.com/gb/en/care/how-much-should-i -water-plant/

How to improve your soil's structure, feed your soil and protect your soil. (n.d.). Lyngso Garden Materials. https://www.lyngsogarden.com /community-resources/how-to-improve-your-soil-structure/

How to increase the pH in soil? (2022, July 18). Atlas Scientific. https://atlas-scientific.com/blog/how-to-increase-the-ph-in-s oil/#:~:text=To%20increase%20the%20pH%20of

How to prepare your garden soil for planting. (2022, May 26). Southern Living. https://www.southernliving.com/garden/how-to-prepar e-garden-soil-for-planting

How to start vegetable seeds indoors. (n.d.). American Meadows. https://www.americanmeadows.com/content/vegetable-gar dening/start-seeds-indoors

Hu, S. (2020, July 20). *Composting 101*. NRDC. https://www.nrdc .org/stories/composting-101#howto

Huffstetler, E. (2019, January 9). *Free printable garden planner*. Www.myfrugalhome.com. https://www.myfrugalhome.com/print able-garden-planner/

Iannotti, M. (2021, July 27). *What is succession planting?* The Spruce. https://www.thespruce.com/succession-planting-1403366

Iannotti, M. (2023, July 11). *9 best flowers for the vegetable garden*. The Spruce. https://www.thespruce.com/flowers-for-the-vegeta ble-garden-1403383

Israel, S. (2021, January 28). *An in-depth companion planting guide*. Www.motherearthnews.com. https://www.motherearthnews.co m/organic-gardening/companion-planting-guide-zmaz81mjzraw/

Jeanroy, A. (2021, July 8). *These 10 easy herbs to grow are perfect for beginners*. The Spruce. https://www.thespruce.com/grow-an-herb-garden-that-wont-die-1762037

Jeanroy, A. (2022, November 11). *Some herbs make poor neighbors*. The Spruce. https://www.thespruce.com/herb-garden-design-mistakes-1762049#:~:text=Chives%20grow%20well%20with%20just

Jill. (2019, February 19). *How to save money gardening: 21 uncommon ideas*. The Beginner's Garden. https://journeywithjill.net/gardening/2019/02/19/how-to-save-money-gardening-21-uncommon-ideas/

Johnson, B. (2013, June 14). *DIY // how to make a garden fence*. Oh everythinghandmade.com. https://oheverythinghandmade.com/diy-how-to-make-a-garden-fence/

Judd, A. (2021, February 4). *5 tips for successful companion planting*. Growing in the Garden. https://growinginthegarden.com/5-tips-for-successful-companion-planting/

Kanuckel, A. (2018, April 25). *Companion planting guide: Sow easy*. Farmers' Almanac. https://www.farmersalmanac.com/companion-planting-guide

Kirsch, M. (2019, June 5). *How to create a simple plant-watering schedule*. Lifehacker. https://lifehacker.com/how-to-create-a-simple-plant-watering-schedule-1833976857

Kosto, A. (2019, June 14). *The science of companion planting in the garden*. Www.montana.edu. https://www.montana.edu/extension/broadwater/blog-article.html?id=18786#:~:text=There%20are%20many%20potential%20benefits

Kuepper, G., & Dodson, M. (2016, January 29). *Companion planting: Basic concepts and resources*. Urban Agriculture Man-

ual. https://urbanagriculture.horticulture.wisc.edu/2016/01/29
/companion-planting-basic-concepts-and-resources/

Lapcevic, K. (2019, February 6). *How to set realistic garden goals.*
Homespun Seasonal Living. https://homespunseasonalliving.co
m/how-to-set-realistic-garden-goals/

Lavezzo, A. (n.d.). *Zone 7 - monthly garden calendar: Chores and
planting   guide.*   Sow   True   Seed.
https://sowtrueseed.com/blogs/monthly-garden-schedule-by-zon
e/zone-7-monthly-garden-calendar-chores-and-planting-guide

Lavezzo, A. (2020a). *Zone 4 - monthly garden calendar: Chores and
planting   guide.*   Sow   True   Seed.
https://sowtrueseed.com/blogs/monthly-garden-schedule-by-zon
e/zone-4-monthly-garden-calendar-chores-and-planting-guide

Lavezzo, A. (2020b). *Zone 5 - monthly garden calendar: Chores and
planting   guide.*   Sow   True   Seed.
https://sowtrueseed.com/blogs/monthly-garden-schedule-by-zon
e/zone-5-monthly-garden-calendar-chores-and-planting-guide#:~:
text=Sow%20seeds%20outdoors%20for%20the

Lavezzo, A. (2020c). *Zone 6 - monthly garden calendar: Chores and
planting   guide.*   Sow   True   Seed.
https://sowtrueseed.com/blogs/monthly-garden-schedule-by-zon
e/zone-6-monthly-garden-calendar-chores-and-planting-guide

Lavezzo, A. (2020d). *Zone 8 - monthly garden calendar: Chores and
planting   guide.*   Sow   True   Seed.
https://sowtrueseed.com/blogs/monthly-garden-schedule-by-zon
e/zone-8-monthly-garden-calendar-chores-and-planting-guide

Lavezzo, A. (2020e). *Zone 9 - monthly garden calendar: Chores and
planting   guide.*   Sow   True   Seed.
https://sowtrueseed.com/blogs/monthly-garden-schedule-by-zon

e/zone-9-monthly-garden-calendar-chores-and-planting-guide#:~:
text=A%20wide%20variety%20of%20herbs

Lavezzo, A. (2020f). *Zone 10 - monthly garden calendar: Chores and planting guide*. Sow True Seed. https://sowtrueseed.com/blogs/monthly-garden-schedule-by-zon e/zone-10-monthly-garden-calendar-chores-and-planting-guide

Lee. (2021, January 1). *How to make toilet paper roll seed starter pots*. Lady Lee's Home. https://ladyleeshome.com/starting-seeds-in-to ilet-paper-rolls/

Lewis, B. (2022, September 22). *Plant these winter cover crops now for better soil in the spring*. Lifehacker. https://lifehacker.com/plant-t hese-winter-cover-crops-now-for-better-soil-in-t-1849564143

Lipford, D. (2010, June 18). *Choosing the right size vegetable garden*. Today's Homeowner. https://todayshomeowner.com/lawn-gard en/guides/choosing-the-right-size-vegetable-garden/

Lisa. (2023, February 19). *How to make an online free garden planner template*. Fluxing Well. https://fluxingwell.com/online-free-gard en-planner/

Lucy. (2023, April 9). *What to plant with cucamelon*. What to Plant With... https://whattoplantwith.com/cucamelons/

Ly, L. (2017, March 1). *Companion planting chart - guide of compatible vegetables*. Gilmour. https://gilmour.com/companion-planting-c hart-guide

MacArthur, A. (2021, December 10). *The best flowers for a vegetable garden to attract pollinators and deter pests*. Food Gardening Network. https://foodgardening.mequoda.com/daily/vegetable-gardening/t he-best-flowers-for-a-vegetable-garden-to-attract-pollinators-and -deter-pests/

Maggie. (2021, December 16). *How I plan out my zone 3 veggie garden*. From Soil to Soul. https://fromsoiltosoul.ca/how-i-plan-out-my -zone-3-veggie-garden/

Magyar, C. (2021, February 11). *Plant spacing - 30 vegetables & their spacing requirements*. Rural Sprout. https://www.ruralsprout.co m/plant-spacing/

Markham, D. (2021, April 6). *8 natural & homemade insecticides: Save your garden without killing the earth*. Treehugger. https://www.treehugger.com/natural-homemade-insecticide s-save-your-garden-without-killing-earth-4858819

Mary. (2022, August 5). *Types and benefits of organic mulching in agriculture*. Geopard.tech. https://geopard.tech/blog/what-is-or ganic-mulching-and-its-benefits/

Maxwell-Gaines, C. (2004, April 4). *Rainwater harvesting 101*. Innovative Water Solutions LLC; Innovative Water Solutions LLC. ht tps://www.watercache.com/education/rainwater-harvesting-101

McCoy, D. (2019, June 4). *Free garden planner printable*. The Rustic Elk. https://www.therusticelk.com/free-garden-planning-pri ntable/

McIndoe, A. (2022, March 3). *Companion planting: Flowers to grow with vegetables*. Learning with Experts. https://www.learningwithexperts.com/gardening/blog/co mpanion-planting-flowers-to-grow-with-vegetables

Mendez, K. A. (2014, April 25). *Tips for saving time in the garden*. FineGardening. https://www.finegardening.com/article/time-sa ving-tips

Miles, J. (2017, May 17). *9 factors to consider when companion planting herbs*. Puffy Carrot. https://puffycarrot.com/companion-plantin g-herbs/

Miller, L. (2024, February 14). *10 common plant diseases (and how to treat them)*. Family Handyman. https://www.familyhandyman.com/list/most-common-plant-diseases/

MNLGrowkits. (2017, June 8). *Water plants twice daily: Early morning and late afternoon*. MNLGrowkits. https://www.mnlgrowkits.com/blogs/articles/water-plants-twice-daily-early-morning-and-late-afternoon

Mock, N. (2022, March 21). *This graphic shows you 20 vegetables you should never grow together*. Taste of Home. https://www.tasteofhome.com/collection/vegetables-you-should-never-grow-together-plus-companion-vegetables/

Mohler, C. L., & Johnson, S. E. (2009a). *Crop rotation and soil tilth*. S A R E . https://www.sare.org/publications/crop-rotation-on-organic-farms/physical-and-biological-processes-in-crop-production/crop-rotation-and-soil-tilth/

Mohler, C. L., & Johnson, S. E. (2009b). *Physical and biological processes in crop production*. SARE. https://www.sare.org/publications/crop-rotation-on-organic-farms/physical-and-biological-processes-in-crop-production/

Montpelier Agway Farm & Garden. (n.d.). Everything you need to know about companion planting. Montpelieragway.com. https://montpelieragway.com/blog/30166/everything-you-need-to-know-about-companion-planting#:~:text=Companion%20planting%20is%20the%20act

Moulton, M. (2022, March 2). *12 sunflower companion plants (& 3 plants to grow nowhere near)*. Blooming Backyard. https://www.bloomingbackyard.com/sunflower-companion-plants/

Mulch calculator - how much mulch do I need? (n.d.). The Calculator Site. https://www.thecalculatorsite.com/construction/mulch-calculator.php

Murray, D. (2020, May 12). *Weird plant tips for your home and garden that actually work*. HGTV Canada. https://www.hgtv.ca/weird-plant-tips-for-your-home-and-garden-that-work/

Neveln, V. (2023, December 13). *How to use hardiness zone information to figure out what you can grow*. Better Homes & Gardens. https://www.bhg.com/gardening/gardening-by-region/how-to-use-hardiness-zone-information/

Nguyen, S. (2022, February 15). *A guide to climate zone 11*. HappySprout. https://www.happysprout.com/inspiration/climate-zone-11-plants/

Nick, J. (2018, July 30). *The pros and cons of square foot gardening*. Good Housekeeping. https://www.goodhousekeeping.com/home/gardening/a20706747/square-foot-gardening/

Nolan, T. (2020, April 7). *4x8 raised bed vegetable garden layout ideas: What to sow & grow*. Savvy Gardening. https://savvygardening.com/4x8-raised-bed-vegetable-garden-layout/

Olly. (2016, March 1). *10 tips to prepare soil for spring*. Envii. https://www.envii.co.uk/garden-blog-post/prepare-soil-for-spring/

Plant disease - symptoms and signs. (n.d.). Encyclopedia Britannica. https://www.britannica.com/science/plant-disease/Symptoms-and-signs

Plant Perfect. (2022, March 28). *How to design the perfect vegetable garden layout*. Plant Perfect. https://plantperfect.com/how-to-design-the-perfect-vegetable-garden-layout/

Plant spacing calculator. (n.d.). The Good Earth Garden Center. https://thegoodearthgarden.com/learning-center/planting-spacing-calculator/

Plants and plant growth chart graphic organizer printout. (n.d.). Ww w.enchantedlearning.com. https://www.enchantedlearning.com /graphicorganizers/plantgrowth/

Rachel. (2020, February 20). *7 simple techniques to improve garden soil*. Grow a Good Life. https://growagoodlife.com/improve-garden-s oil/

Rakes, M. (2020, May 14). *15 money-saving gardening tips that will save you hundreds*. Graceful Little Honey Bee. https://www.gracefullittlehoneybee.com/15-money-saving -tips-from-a-frugal-gardener/

Reynolds, M. (2021, December 10). *Spring growing chart*. Territorial Seed. https://territorialseed.com/blogs/spring-growing-guides /spring-growing-chart

Richmond, J. (2021, March 1). *How plants use water*. Extension. https://extension.wvu.edu/lawn-gardening-pests/news/202 1/03/01/how-plants-use-water

Riotte, L. (2004). *Carrots love tomatoes & roses love garlic: Secrets of companion planting for successful gardening*. Storey.

Sansone, A. (2020, April 30). *The easiest way to calculate how much mulch your garden needs*. Country Living. https://www.countryliving.com/gardening/garden-ideas/a2 6029780/how-much-mulch-do-i-need/

Schiller, N. (2022, January 1). *23 beneficial insects & creepy crawlies great for your garden*. Gardener's Path. https://gardenerspath.co m/how-to/disease-and-pests/beneficial-insects/

Science Learning Hub. (2013, July 30). *Soil properties*. Science Learning Hub; Science Learning Hub. https://www.sciencelearn.org.n z/resources/957-soil-properties

Selemin, J. (2022, November 25). *Benefits of companion planting*. WebMD. https://www.webmd.com/a-to-z-guides/benefits-of-co mpanion-planting

7 pro tips for fall soil preparation you should know about. (2021, September 28). McCarty Mulch. https://www.landscapemulch.com /blog/7-pro-tips-for-fall-soil-preparation/

Shinn, M. (2020, July 27). *Planting in threes explained, and when to break the rule*. Horticulture. https://www.hortmag.com/gardens /planting-in-threes

Shinn, M. (2022, January 31). Time saving tips for indoor seed starting. *Horticulture*. https://www.hortmag.com/smart-gardening/ti me-saving-tips-seeds

Siegel, S. (2020, July 13). *10 natural ways to eliminate garden insect pests*. Birds and Blooms. https://www.birdsandblooms.com/gardening/gardenin g-basics/natural-ways-eliminate-garden-insect-pests/

Soil calculator - calculate soil for garden beds and potting containers. (n.d.). Soilcalculator.com. https://soilcalculator.com/

Soil health management. (n.d.). Www.keralasoilfertility.net. https:// www.keralasoilfertility.net/en/soil_health_management.jsp

Succession planting - all you need to know. (2023, November 30). AllThatGrows. https://www.allthatgrows.in/blogs/posts/succes sion-planting-guide

Talerico, D. (2020, March 9). *Companion planting 101 (w/ garden companion planting chart)*. Homestead and Chill. https://home steadandchill.com/benefits-companion-planting-chart/

Thomas, J. (2023, April 17). *Companion planting in the vegetable garden*. Homesteading Family. https://homesteadingfamily.com/companion-planting-in-the-veg

etable-garden/#:~:text=The%20Three%20Sisters%20companion
%20planting

3- zone 1 garden. (n.d.). Www.ficustemple.com. https://www.ficust
emple.com/permaculture/3-zone-1-garden

Tilley,   N.   (2022,   November   22). *Choosing   the   size
of   your   vegetable   garden.*   Www.gardeningknowhow.com
. https://www.gardeningknowhow.com/edible/vegetables/vgen/
choosing-the-size-of-your-vegetable-garden.htm

Tips & information about ideas & inspiration. (n.d.). Gardeningknowhow. https://www.gardeningknowhow.com/ideas-inspirati
on

Toney, S. (2014, January 11). *16 ways to use companion planting for
pest control naturally.* The Free Range Life®. https://thefreerang
elife.com/companion-planting-to-control-pests-naturally/

Tonoli, M. (2017, September 26). *Companion planting principles.*
Meadow Sweet. https://meadowsweet.co.nz/2017/09/26/compa
nion-planting-principles/

Top 10 easy to grow flower plants and seeds for beginners. (2019). Tho
mpson-Morgan.com. https://www.thompson-morgan.com/top
-10-easy-to-grow-flowers

Top 10 tips for saving money in the garden. (n.d.). Www.thompson
-Morgan.com. https://www.thompson-morgan.com/top-10-mo
ney-saving-tips-garden

*Topsoil, dirt & mulch bulk material calculator | calculate how much
topsoil you need cubic yards.* (n.d.). Www.lestersmaterial.com.
https://www.lestersmaterial.com/Bulk-Material-Cubic-Yard-Ton
-Calculator/Bulk-Mulch-Topsoil-Material-Calculator#:~:text=Le
ngth%20in%20feet%20x%20Width

Toscano,   K.   (2022,   March   28). *Proper   plant
spacing   and   why   it   matters.*   Worx   Toolshed

Blog. https://www.worx.com/blog/proper-plant-spacing-and-why-it-matters/#:~:text=The%20easy%20way%20to%20determine

20 unusual gardening tips that work. (2014, August 12). Install It Direct. https://www.installitdirect.com/learn/unusual-gardening-tips-that-work/

Types of soil. (2018, July 5). BYJUS; Byju's. https://byjus.com/biology/types-of-soil/

USDA. (2020). *USDA plant hardiness zone map.* United States Department of Agriculture. https://planthardiness.ars.usda.gov/

Utilizing nasturtiums companion plants for natural pest control. (2024, February 29). Meadowlark Journal. https://meadowlarkjournal.com/blog/nasturtiums-companion-plants#:~:text=Planting%20nasturtiums%20as%20companions%20to

Vanderlinden, C. (2023, June 6). *Cucumber companion plants: What's good, bad, and best.* The Spruce. https://www.thespruce.com/companion-plants-for-cucumbers-2540044#:~:text=Best%20Companion%20Plants%20for%20Cucumbers&text=Peas%2C%20corn%2C%20beans%2C%20and

Vanheems, B. (2017, July 9). *Cover crops to recharge your soil this winter!* GrowVeg. https://www.growveg.com/guides/cover-crops-to-recharge-your-soil-this-winter/

vic. (2017, September 29). *8 gardening tools you need.* KYK Tools Philippines. https://kyk.com.ph/blog/gardening-tools-needed/

Vinje, E. (2018, November 5). *How to prepare garden soil for planting.* Planet Natural. https://www.planetnatural.com/garden-soil/

Waterworth, K. (2022, September 26). *11 common garden pests to look out for this year.* Forbes Home. https://www.forbes.com/home-improvement/pest-control/common-garden-pests/

Waterworth, K. (2023, May 2). *Incompatible garden plants: Learn about plants that don't like each other.* Www.gardeningknowhow .com. https://www.gardeningknowhow.com/edible/vegetables/v gen/incompatible-garden-plants.htm

Wells, K. (2023, May 12). *How to grow a better garden with companion planting.* Wellness Mama®. https://wellnessmama.com/natural -home/companion-planting/

What is pruning? Importance, benefits & methods of pruning. (n.d.). Blog.davey.com. https://blog.davey.com/what-is-pruning-the-im portance-benefits-and-methods-of-pruning/

What is the importance of water for plants. (n.d.). Byjus.com . https://byjus.com/question-answer/what-is-the-importance-of -water-for-plants/

What vegetables to plant in zone 6. (n.d.). Hyper-Grow.com. https:/ /hyper-grow.com/news/what-vegetables-to-plant-in-zone-6/

Why is companion planting so important? (2023, June 19). Triangle Gardener. https://www.trianglegardener.com/why-is-compa nion-planting-so-important/

Wiley, D. (2022, August 27). *Why you need to start vertical gardening now.* Better Homes & Gardens. https://www.bhg.com/gardenin g/container/plans-ideas/vertical-gardening/

Woita, M. (2024, January 1). *Garden planning + seed starting dates for zone 5 growers.* Boots & Hooves Homestead. https://bootsandho oveshomestead.com/how-to-plan-a-garden-in-zone-5/

Young, M. (2019, November 2). *7 quick composting tips to help you save valuable time.* Farm Fit Living. https://farmfitliving.com/7-quic k-composting-tips-to-help-you-save-valuable-time/

Zone 1 vegetable planting guide. (n.d.). Mary's Heirloom Seeds. https://www.marysheirloomseeds.com/blogs/news/zone -1-vegetable-planting-guide

Zone 8 plants - find the best plants for hardiness zone 8. (n.d.). Www. brecks.com. https://www.brecks.com/category/zone8/a#:~:text= Asters%2C%20astilbe%2C%20bee%20balm%2C

Zone 10 plants - the best plants for hardiness zone 10. (n.d.). Www.b recks.com. https://www.brecks.com/category/zone10/a#:~:text= Cannas%2C%20croton%2C%20dahlias%2C%20geraniums

Made in United States
Cleveland, OH
04 November 2024

10470274R00109